ARTIFICIAL INTELLIGENCE AND THE HUMAN SPARK

Humanity at the Crossroads

Embracing Collaboration, Innovation and a Human-Centered Future

SNEHANSHU JENA

Email: hello@snehanshu.in

Website: www.snehanshu.in

Snehanshu Jena

Copyright © 2025 by Snehanshu Jena

TABLE OF CONTENTS

INTRODUCTION   **5**

My Journey Through A World Being Rewritten By AI   5

THE AI REVOLUTION AND THE QUESTION OF HUMANITY   **12**

AI Permeating Daily Life and work   18

The Fundamental Question   24

Addressing Initial Anxieties & Misconceptions   29

Moving Beyond the Narrative of Replacement   34

THE AGE OF AUGMENTED CONTRIBUTION   **39**

Reframing the Economic and Societal Impact of AI   43

Enhancing Human Capabilities with AI   49

Enabling New Forms of Value Creation   53

Human Ingenuity, Creativity and Critical Thinking   58

The Synergy of Human Skills Augmented by AI   65

Embracing Future - Technology as a Human Amplifier   74

DEFINING HUMANITY NOW   **79**

The Timeless Question   83

Exploring Human Dimensions   87

Ancient Wisdom on Human Existence   94

Existentialism and Humanism   100

The Shared Human Condition   106

Attributes That Truly Distinguish   112

CONCLUSION - AI VS. HUMAN CONSCIOUSNESS — 119

THE ENIGMA OF CONSCIOUSNESS — 120

THE SPARK OF HUMAN CREATIVITY — 121

THE DEPTH OF HUMAN EMPATHY — 122

THE NUANCES OF HUMAN CRITICAL THINKING — 123

THE INTERPLAY AND ENDURING IMPORTANCE — 124

WHAT'S NEXT? — 125

REFERENCES — 128

DISCLAIMER — 130

MAY I ASK YOU A SMALL FAVOUR? — 131

INTRODUCTION

MY JOURNEY THROUGH A WORLD BEING REWRITTEN BY AI

My career has taken quite a few unexpected turns and looking back, it all started in an automotive manufacturing plant. Right there, amidst the energy of the production line, my focus was on the fundamental aspects of making things. This hands-on experience laid the foundation for my exploration into a question that has now become central to our time: what does it mean to be human in an age increasingly shaped by artificial intelligence?

Back then every day was about ensuring the well-being of my team – their safety was paramount. We were also driven by the need to produce high-quality products that people could rely on. Meeting our delivery schedules was crucial to keep things moving smoothly. Of course, we were always mindful of cost efficiency, making sure our operations were sustainable. And a happy team, good morale, was essential for everyone's success. Lastly, we were increasingly aware of our impact on the environment.

These six areas – Safety, Quality, Delivery, Cost, Morale and Environment – became more than just targets; they formed the bedrock of how I approached any task. You could say it became a way of thinking, a lens through which I viewed every process and every decision. For instance, when we were considering new equipment for my line, the first questions weren't just about speed, but about whether it was safe for the people and if it would result in a better, more reliable product.

Would it help us get the product to our customers on time? Would it be a cost-effective solution in the long run? Would it improve the work experience for those involved? And what would be its impact on our resource consumption and waste?

In the initial years in Manufacturing, I had short term assignments in sales and services, out in the field, meeting people and understanding their needs. After that, it was all about how things moved, the flow of supply chains, trying to make everything run smoothly. But deep down, I always had this drive to learn more, to understand the bigger picture, which eventually led me into the world of making decisions in manufacturing, transitioning to planning and then to IT roles as SME (Subject Matter Expert), leading & architecting cloud solutions and managing teams.

Looking back, those experiences were all about understanding how things work, the nitty-gritty details of processes and people. But now, things are changing faster than ever before and the biggest shift I've seen is the rise of artificial intelligence or AI. It's not just some futuristic idea anymore; it's here, it's real and it's changing everything around us, from the way we work to the way we live.

For over fifteen years, I was deeply involved in the automotive industry. It's worth noting that cars are more than just metal and engines now. They're becoming computers on wheels, filled with technology. I saw how automation was changing manufacturing, how engineering was using new digital tools and how even the supply chain was getting smarter. That gave me a front-row seat to the early days of this technological shift - from IT being limited to office desks and networks needed for the machines in the plant to its pivotal role with the rise of Web, Cloud and AI.

Then a few years ago I made a big jump to BigTech. It was like stepping into a whole new world, right at the heart of where AI is being developed and used in ways I couldn't have fully imagined before. This journey, from the nuts and bolts of car manufacturing, to leading Manufacturing Cloud projects and then to the cutting edge of AI, has given me a unique perspective on what this all means for us as humans.

What I've come to realize is that this AI revolution isn't about some dystopian future where machines take over. Instead, I see it as a tremendous opportunity to make us, as humans, even better, to amplify our inherent capabilities. And when I consider this potential, my mind still goes back to those fundamental principles from the shop floor.

When we think about AI as a powerful technology, much like a more sophisticated piece of equipment on a production line, the same questions apply. Will AI-powered systems augment human capabilities to create safer workplaces by handling hazardous tasks? Will they lead to higher quality products and services through better analysis and precision? Can they improve delivery and efficiency by optimizing processes and providing real-time insights, acting like an experienced navigator guiding us to our goals? Will they contribute to more sustainable costs in the long run by automating repetitive tasks and optimizing resource allocation? How will the integration of AI affect team morale?

Will it free us from mundane work and allow us to focus on more engaging and creative endeavors? And crucially, what will be the environmental impact of these technologies in terms of energy consumption and resource utilization? Just as we need building codes to ensure physical safety, we need to address the ethical and practical guidelines for AI development and deployment to ensure its safe and beneficial use.

This is why I wanted to write this book – to explore this evolving relationship between us and AI, not from a perspective of fear, but from one of optimism and possibility, always keeping in mind those foundational principles that have guided my thinking throughout my professional life.

Consider what's happening with technology. We have these incredibly smart systems, like the ones that can write complex text, compose music, even help with scientific research. It can feel like these machines are starting to do everything we used to think was distinctly human. So "How do we define humanity with the rise of AI?" This isn't a new question, of course. People have been pondering the meaning of life and what makes us human for centuries. But AI adds a whole new layer to this discussion. We need to look at what makes us who we are – our biology, our societies, how we think and how we feel – in the context of these increasingly smart machines.

One of the things that really excites me is the idea that AI can actually help us become more capable. It's not about replacing us, but about boosting our abilities. For example, think about people with disabilities. AI is already making a huge difference with things like more precise prosthetic limbs that they can control with their minds or systems that let people with speech difficulties communicate more easily. There's even talk about future technologies that could help improve our memory or focus. These aren't just science fiction dreams; they're becoming realities.

I remember reading about Industry 5.0 and it really struck a chord with me. It's this idea that the future of manufacturing and many other industries, isn't just about more automation. It's about combining human creativity with advanced technology. It's about finding that sweet spot where machines handle the repetitive and data-heavy tasks, freeing us up to focus on the things that truly require human ingenuity and problem-solving.

As I've seen recently, the power of AI to analyze vast amounts of information is incredible. It can spot patterns and insights that we humans might miss. This can lead to better decisions in all sorts of fields, from business strategy to medical diagnoses. It's like having a super-smart assistant that can process information at lightning speed, helping us make more informed choices. But it's not just about thinking faster or analyzing more data. AI is also helping us communicate better. Think about translation tools that can instantly bridge language barriers, making it easier for people from different cultures to connect and understand each other. This can lead to more inclusive and collaborative environments, both in our personal lives and in the global workforce.

Of course, with all this amazing potential comes a lot of important questions and even some worries. We need to make sure that as we develop and use AI, we're doing it in a way that's fair and equitable for everyone. We need to address the bias in the data that AI learns from and how to make sure everyone has access to these powerful tools. Privacy and data security are also huge concerns. We must build these systems responsibly, with ethical guidelines.

Having navigated the challenges of industry and now witnessing the power of cutting-edge technology, I'm convinced that our humanity is paramount. AI excels in many areas, but it lacks the creative spark, emotional resonance and intuitive judgment that define us. These are the qualities we must prioritize and celebrate in the era of advanced machines.

We are going to take a deep dive into all of this. We'll explore how AI is changing our cognitive abilities – things like intelligence, memory and focus – and the potential upsides and downsides. We'll also look at how AI is impacting our social and emotional development, including our communication and social skills. It's crucial to talk about the ethics of all this. How do we ensure fairness and equity as AI becomes more integrated into our lives? How do we protect our privacy and maintain control over these powerful systems? These are questions we need to tackle together. But it's not all challenges. I also want to explore how AI can help us build a more just and equitable society. By closing data gaps, reducing bias in decision-making and improving access to essential services, AI has the potential to be a real force for good.

Ultimately, this book is about navigating this incredible new era with our humanity intact, even enhanced. It's about understanding how AI can be a powerful partner, helping us achieve more and focus on what truly makes life meaningful. It's about embracing the "Age of Augmented Contribution," where technology frees us to be more creative, more innovative and more human.

THE AI REVOLUTION AND THE QUESTION OF HUMANITY

AI is not new but recent events like - Google open-sourced Transformers in 2017 followed by the ChatGPT and Deepseek moments, has ushered in a technological transformation unlike any seen before. This isn't just a minor upgrade to existing technology; it's a fundamental shift, often referred to as the AI Revolution. At the heart of this revolution are sophisticated forms of AI - most notably Generative AI and Large Language Models (LLMs). These technologies are not mere theoretical concepts confined to research laboratories; they are increasingly woven into the fabric of our daily lives and reshaping the operations of industries across the globe. This pervasive influence of AI compels us to confront a profound and age-old question with renewed urgency: in a world increasingly shaped by intelligent machines, what remains unique to humans as AI develops?

This rapid evolution, while promising, also raises fundamental questions about the safety and reliability (quality) of these new AI models in widespread use. Let's look into what makes them so revolutionary. Think of Generative AI as an AI that can create new original content. It's like having a digital assistant with a wide range of creative talents. Unlike older forms of AI that primarily focused on analyzing existing data or automating specific tasks, Generative AI has learned patterns from vast datasets and can use that knowledge to produce entirely new outputs. This could be anything from writing a poem or a news article to designing a product, composing music or even generating realistic images and videos. We can describe Generative AI as a partner in creative endeavors highlighting its role in helping us produce novel creations. For example, imagine an artist using AI tools to explore new artistic styles or generate initial sketches or a musician using AI to experiment with different melodies and harmonies. This capability moves AI beyond mere automation into the realm of creation and innovation. LLMs are a specific type of Generative AI that focuses on understanding and generating human language. A simple yet insightful analogy, will be to consider LLMs as "Autocomplete on overdrive". While your phone's autocomplete suggests the next word as you type, LLMs operate on a much grander scale. They have been trained on massive amounts of text and code, allowing them to understand context, nuances and even different writing styles. This enables them to perform a wide array of language-based tasks, such as answering complex questions, translating languages, writing different kinds of creative content, summarizing long documents and even engaging in seemingly natural conversations. The fact that LLMs can generate human language in a way that sometimes feels indistinguishable from human writing is one of the key factors driving the current wave of excitement and also apprehension surrounding AI.

As mentioned, these powerful AI technologies are no longer confined to the sterile environments of research labs. They are rapidly spreading throughout various facets of our daily lives and the intricate operations of industries. Think about your daily interactions with technology. If you've ever used a virtual assistant on your smartphone, received personalized recommendations while shopping online or interacted with a customer service chatbot, you've likely encountered AI. We have non-human Customer Service Reps which illustrates how AI is becoming the first point of contact for many customer service inquiries, offering quick answers and support much like a human representative.

The impact of AI is equally profound in the industrial sector. In manufacturing, AI is being integrated into processes to enhance efficiency, improve quality control and even predict equipment failures before they happen. Consider the concept of "intelligent and resilient supply chains". AI, along with technologies like Large Language Models (LLMs), Digital Twins and the Internet of Things (IoT), is transforming how goods are sourced, manufactured and delivered. AI can analyze vast amounts of data to optimize logistics, predict potential disruptions and ensure that supply chains are not only efficient but also capable of withstanding unexpected challenges. This application of AI demonstrates its potential to create more robust and adaptable industrial operations.

Furthermore, the vision of "Smart Cities as Intelligent Ecosystems" illustrates how AI could revolutionize urban living. In this concept, technology is integrated into every aspect of city life to improve efficiency, sustainability and the overall quality of life for residents. AI could manage traffic flow, optimize energy consumption, enhance public safety and even personalize public services.

The widespread adoption of AI across these diverse domains signifies that it's not just a niche technology but a fundamental force reshaping how we live and work. The increasing capabilities and pervasiveness of AI naturally lead us to a profound and practical question: what fundamentally defines humanity in a world where machines can perform tasks that were once considered the exclusive domain of human intellect?

For centuries, human beings have often defined their uniqueness, at least in part, by their intellectual superiority. Our capacity for complex thought, reasoning, creativity and problem-solving has been seen as a key differentiator between humans and the rest of the natural world. However, the emergence of intelligent machines that can now exhibit behaviors mimicking these very capabilities challenges this long-held belief. As AI systems become proficient in tasks like writing sophisticated text, composing music and even conducting scientific research, it compels us to re-evaluate what truly sets us apart. The very notion of machine intelligence challenges our long-held beliefs about human uniqueness, which have often been predicated on our perceived intellectual superiority.

Exploring the essence of being a Human - isn't merely an abstract philosophical debate; it has significant implications for how we understand ourselves and our place in the evolving technological landscape. As intelligent machines become more integrated into our lives and industries, we are forced to examine the core essence of our being. What are the attributes that truly distinguish humans from even the most advanced AI systems?

Philosophical perspectives suggest that AI's significance extends beyond mere automation. The very existence of machine intelligence forces us to confront the nature of intelligence itself. While AI systems can now perform tasks that might be labeled as intelligent when done by humans, the question remains whether this constitutes genuine thought or simply sophisticated mimicry. Some argue that true intelligence is intrinsically linked to consciousness and subjective experience – the feeling of being aware – qualities that are not currently attributed to machines. Others contend that if a machine can perform intellectual tasks indistinguishably from a human, then it should, in essence, be considered intelligent. This ongoing debate highlights the difficulty in definitively drawing a line between human and artificial intellect.

There are several facets of human existence that contribute to our understanding of what it means to be human. Consciousness, the subjective awareness of oneself and one's surroundings, is often cited as a crucial differentiator. Humans possess the capacity for introspection, self-awareness and the experience of qualia – the subjective "feel" of things like the color blue or the taste of chocolate. Creativity, the ability to generate novel and valuable ideas or artifacts, is another hallmark of human intelligence. While AI is increasingly capable of generating creative outputs, the underlying drive, intentionality and emotional resonance often remain human in nature.

Furthermore, qualities like empathy – the ability to understand and share the feelings of others – intuition and nuanced critical thinking that goes beyond pure logic and data analysis are also often considered core to being human. It also emphasizes the rich and complex landscape of human emotions, from joy and love to sorrow and fear, which shape our perceptions and drive our actions in ways that contrast with the more logical and data-driven processes of AI. The intricate interplay between emotions and reason in human thought and behavior is a defining characteristic.

Beyond the capacity for intelligent thought and creative output, what inherent attributes truly distinguish human beings from advanced AI systems? Understanding what we believe is fundamentally human can guide us in several key areas:

• The Future of Work: By identifying the skills and qualities that remain exclusive, we can better understand the roles that humans will continue to play in the workforce and where our focus should lie in terms of education and training.

• Education and Skill Development: Recognizing the enduring value of human traits like creativity, critical thinking and emotional intelligence can inform how we design educational systems to cultivate these qualities in future generations.

• Ethical AI Development: Our understanding of human values and what makes us human can help guide the ethical development and deployment of AI technologies, ensuring that they align with human well-being and societal good.

- Our Relationship with Technology: By reflecting on what defines our humanity, we can foster a more balanced and human-centric relationship with AI, viewing it as a tool to augment our capabilities rather than a replacement for our very essence.

The increasing interaction with AI might paradoxically lead to a renewed appreciation and focus on these traits. As machines take over more routine and analytical tasks, humans may find themselves with more time and space to cultivate their creativity, empathy and critical thinking skills. This shift could lead to a re-evaluation of what aspects of work and life are most meaningful and inherently human. By acknowledging the profound ways in which AI is shaping our world and by thoughtfully considering the essence of our own being, we can navigate this technological transformation in a way that not only preserves but also enhances what makes us human. The journey into the age of intelligent machines is also a journey of self-discovery, prompting us to appreciate the enduring value of our consciousness and nuanced critical thinking.

AI PERMEATING DAILY LIFE AND WORK

Artificial intelligence is rapidly moving beyond the realm of science fiction and specialized technology sectors to become a subtle yet powerful force in our everyday routines and the fundamental operations of industries worldwide or our work. This integration is often so seamless that we might not consciously register the presence of AI, yet it is quietly reshaping how we live, interact with technology and conduct business.

Think about the simple act of finding your way to a new restaurant. Many of us now rely on applications on our smartphones that provide turn-by-turn directions. These digital guides utilize AI at their core. They analyze a multitude of data points, including real-time traffic flow, road closures and even accident reports, to calculate the most efficient route to your destination. This AI acts like an experienced navigator, constantly reassessing conditions and suggesting alternative paths to save you time and frustration. It's as if you have a knowledgeable co-pilot for every journey, making travel smoother and more predictable.

Consider the way we enjoy music. For millions, music streaming services have become the primary way to listen to our favorite artists and discover new ones. These services employ AI as a personalized DJ. By tracking your listening habits, the songs you skip or replay and the playlists you create, the AI learns your musical tastes. It then uses this knowledge to recommend new tracks and artists you might enjoy, curating personalized radio stations and discovery playlists. This AI DJ acts like a friend with impeccable taste, always knowing the perfect song to play next.

Our homes are also becoming increasingly intelligent, thanks to the integration of AI. Smart home devices can now manage various aspects of our living spaces, from adjusting the thermostat and turning on lights to securing our property and even operating kitchen appliances, often in response to voice commands or learned preferences. This AI acts like a helpful, attentive butler, anticipating your needs and managing your home environment for comfort and convenience.

The way we shop has also been profoundly influenced by AI. Online retailers utilize AI as a virtual personal shopper. As you browse their websites, AI algorithms analyze your clicks, the items you view and your purchase history to understand your interests and preferences. Based on this analysis, the AI recommends products you might like, often presenting them in personalized sections of the website or in targeted emails. It's like having a knowledgeable sales assistant who understands your style and can point you towards exactly what you're looking for, even before you knew you wanted it.

Even our interactions on social media are shaped by AI. The feeds we see are not simply chronological lists of updates from our connections. Instead, AI acts as a curator, filtering and prioritizing the vast amounts of content generated daily. These algorithms analyze your past interactions, the types of posts you engage with and the content shared by your network to present you with a feed that is designed to be relevant and engaging, increasing the likelihood that you'll spend more time on the platform.

When we seek assistance from customer service, we might find ourselves interacting with AI in the form of chatbots. These AI-powered problem solvers are designed to answer frequently asked questions, provide information about products or services and even resolve basic issues. They can offer instant support at any time, acting as a first line of response and often handling inquiries efficiently without the need for human intervention. This is AI acting as an ever-available and patient customer service representative.

Furthermore, AI is breaking down communication barriers through language translation tools. These systems can instantly translate text and speech between different languages, facilitating communication across cultures and enabling people from around the world to understand each other more easily. This AI acts like a multilingual communication facilitator, making global interactions more seamless.

In the realm of creativity, AI is emerging as a collaborative assistant. Tools powered by AI can help artists, writers and musicians generate ideas, explore new styles and even produce initial drafts of content. While human oversight and artistry remain crucial, AI can act as a powerful brainstorming partner and a tool to amplify creative potential.

Beyond our individual experiences, AI is revolutionizing the way industries operate, driving efficiency, innovation and resilience. In manufacturing, AI is acting as an incredibly precise quality controller. AI-powered visual inspection systems can meticulously examine products on assembly lines, identifying even minute defects that might be missed by human eyes. This leads to higher quality products, reduced waste and more consistent manufacturing standards.

AI is also taking on the role of a proactive maintenance technician. By continuously analyzing data from sensors embedded in machinery, AI algorithms can detect subtle patterns that indicate potential equipment failures. This allows maintenance teams to schedule repairs and replacements proactively, minimizing unexpected downtime and ensuring smoother and more reliable production processes. It's like having a predictive maintenance expert constantly monitoring the health of the machinery.

The complex world of supply chains is also being transformed by AI, which acts as an intelligent logistics optimizer. AI algorithms can analyze vast datasets related to transportation, warehousing, demand forecasting and potential disruptions to identify the most efficient routes, schedules and inventory levels. This leads to faster delivery times, reduced transportation costs and more resilient supply networks that can better adapt to unforeseen challenges. Imagine AI as a highly skilled supply chain manager orchestrating the flow of goods with exceptional precision. The concept of "intelligent supply chains" underscores how AI enhances visibility and collaboration across the entire network. Large Language Models can further aid in this by streamlining communication and information flow between different stakeholders.

Within warehouses and logistics centers, AI is powering a new generation of collaborative robots. These AI-driven machines can navigate autonomously and work alongside human employees to automate tasks such as transporting materials, picking and packing orders and managing inventory. This collaboration enhances efficiency, reduces the physical burden on human workers and minimizes errors. It's a partnership where AI handles repetitive or physically demanding tasks, allowing humans to focus on more complex and strategic activities.

The automotive industry is undergoing a profound transformation driven by the adoption of Software-Defined Vehicles (SDVs) and Digital Twins, with AI playing a central role. Digital Twins, which are virtual replicas of vehicles or manufacturing processes, allow for simulations and optimizations in a virtual environment before any physical prototypes are built. Generative AI can further accelerate this process by rapidly creating numerous design variations and predicting the most effective configurations based on performance and efficiency metrics. This integration of AI and virtual technologies is leading to faster development cycles, more innovative designs and the ability to customize vehicles to an unprecedented degree.

Even in the initial stages of product creation, AI is becoming an invaluable design assistant. Generative AI tools can help designers explore a wide range of design possibilities, generate multiple iterations based on specific requirements and even optimize designs for factors like cost-effectiveness and manufacturability. This allows for a more rapid and creative design process, leading to the development of more innovative and efficient products across various industries.

Across the industrial landscape, AI is being incorporated into technologies that augment human capabilities. AI-powered analytics can meticulously examine mountains of data or massive datasets far more efficiently than humans, providing valuable insights that can inform critical business decisions. AI can also automate routine administrative tasks, freeing up human employees to focus on more strategic, creative and complex aspects of their work. Wearable devices equipped with AI can monitor workers' safety in real-time, detecting potential hazards and providing alerts to prevent accidents. Similarly, AI-driven ergonomic monitoring systems can analyze workers' movements and postures to provide feedback that helps prevent musculoskeletal injuries, contributing to a healthier and more productive workforce.

This widespread integration of AI into both our daily lives and the core operations of industries signifies a major shift. It's not merely about automation in the traditional sense; it's about the emergence of intelligent systems that can learn, adapt and collaborate with humans to enhance our capabilities and drive progress across numerous domains. As AI continues to evolve, its presence will likely become even more pervasive, further blurring the lines between the digital and physical worlds and reshaping the future of how we live and work together.

THE FUNDAMENTAL QUESTION

The increasing presence and capability of artificial intelligence in our world compels us to look inwards and ask a very fundamental question: what is it that truly makes us human? As AI becomes more sophisticated, capable of performing tasks that we once believed were exclusive to human intellect, our understanding of our own uniqueness is being challenged. For a long time, our intellectual prowess has been a cornerstone of our self-perception. We have seen ourselves as the most intelligent beings on this planet and this intellectual superiority has often been considered a defining characteristic of humanity. However, the emergence of technology that can analyze vast amounts of data, solve complex problems and even exhibit creativity in certain domains is prompting a re-evaluation of this viewpoint.

This inquiry into the essence of humanity in an AI-shaped world is not just an abstract philosophical exercise. It carries significant weight and has tangible implications for how we navigate the future. Our understanding of what we consider fundamentally human will influence the roles we prioritize in our societies, the way we approach education and personal development and even the principles that guide the design and implementation of AI systems. Ultimately, it will help us determine how we can best complement and enhance our human capabilities in a world increasingly populated by intelligent machines.

Thinking about what sets us apart, even as AI advances, brings to mind several qualities that currently seem to be human in nature. One of these is consciousness – that inner awareness, the subjective experience of being alive and perceiving the world around us. It's the feeling of what it's like to see a sunset, to feel joy or to experience sorrow. This inner life, this "ghost in the machine" or "spark of life," remains a profound mystery and whether AI can ever truly possess it is a question that continues to be debated.

Another deeply human trait is creativity, especially when it arises from genuine intention and emotion. While AI can generate novel outputs, the underlying drive, the personal motivation and the emotional resonance that often fuel human creativity seem to be different. Think of an artist pouring their heart into a painting or a musician composing a melody that expresses a deep feeling. This kind of creativity feels intrinsically linked to our human experience. AI can act as a "muse" - inspiring and assisting, but the core intent often originates from human emotion and perspective.

Then there is empathy, the ability to understand and share the feelings of others. It's the capacity to connect with someone on an emotional level, to recognize their joys and sorrows and to respond with compassion. This ability is fundamental to our social interactions and moral reasoning. While AI can be programmed to recognize and respond to emotional cues, replicating the genuine understanding and shared experience of empathy is a significant challenge.

Our capacity for critical thinking also stands out. It involves not just processing information but also analyzing it objectively, evaluating different arguments and forming reasoned judgments. This often involves contextual understanding and intuition, drawing on a wealth of life experiences and knowledge that goes beyond pure data analysis. While AI excels at processing vast amounts of data, the nuanced application of critical thought, especially in ambiguous or novel situations, often remains a human strength.

Furthermore, humans are inherently social beings and our ability to connect with each other, to communicate effectively and to build complex relationships is a defining aspect of our humanity. This involves a rich interplay of verbal and nonverbal cues, often relying on unspoken understanding and shared context. AI can help us connect across distances, "breaking down walls" in communication and even act as "practice partners" for social skills, but the depth and complexity of genuine human interaction, driven by empathy and shared experiences, remain distinctive.

Our emotional landscape also contributes significantly to what it means to be human. Emotions shape our perceptions, drive our actions and play a crucial role in our decision-making processes and relationships. They are complex and often not purely logical, yet they provide valuable information about our internal state and the world around us. AI can act as a "mirror," helping us understand our own emotions better, but the intricate and often seemingly irrational nature of human emotions is a fundamental aspect of our experience that goes beyond mere data processing.

The concept of free will, the sense of choice and control over our actions, is another area that distinguishes us. While AI operates based on its programming, humans possess a subjective sense of agency and the ability to make choices that are not solely determined by prior inputs. The extent of our free will is a long-standing philosophical debate, but our lived experience of making choices feels inherently human, like a "butterfly in the wind," influenced by many factors but still charting its own course.

Even in areas where AI shows great promise, like memory and learning, there are some unique aspects. AI can augment our memory, acting like a "digital brain" to help us remember vast amounts of information. And AI excels at personalized learning, acting like a "private tutor" adapting to individual needs. However, human memory is often tied to personal experiences, emotions and the context in which events occurred, adding layers of meaning and connection that go beyond mere data storage and retrieval.

Our ability to learn and use language also highlights our human uniqueness. AI can process and generate language with impressive fluency, even acting as a "language buddy" to help us learn new languages. But human language is deeply intertwined with culture, emotion and nuanced understanding that goes beyond grammatical rules and vocabulary.

Interestingly, as AI becomes more integrated into our lives, it might paradoxically lead to a renewed appreciation and focus on these very human qualities. As machines take over more routine and analytical tasks, we may find ourselves with more time and space to cultivate our creativity, empathy, critical thinking and social skills. This shift could lead to a re-evaluation of what aspects of work and life are most meaningful and inherently human. The integration of AI has the potential to free us from mundane tasks, allowing us to concentrate on activities that require imagination, emotional intelligence and complex problem-solving – areas where our capabilities remain distinctly advantageous.

Ultimately, the question of what constitutes humanity in an AI-shaped world is not about defining ourselves in opposition to machines but rather about understanding and appreciating the unique essence of our being. While AI can undoubtedly augment and transform our capabilities, the core attributes of consciousness, creativity, empathy, nuanced critical thinking, rich social connections and complex emotions continue to define what it means to be human in this evolving technological landscape. By recognizing and nurturing these qualities, we can navigate the age of intelligent machines not with fear of obsolescence, but with a focus on amplified human flourishing, embracing AI as an enabler that helps us realize our full potential. This concept of amplified human contribution will see us working in partnership with AI, leveraging its strengths while cherishing and developing the unique attributes that make us, fundamentally, human.

ADDRESSING INITIAL ANXIETIES & MISCONCEPTIONS

It's very understandable that the rise of powerful artificial intelligence can create a sense of unease and bring up several worries in people's minds. When we hear about machines becoming increasingly capable, taking on tasks that once required human skills, it's natural to feel a bit anxious about what this means for our future. One of the most prominent of these initial anxieties revolves around the prospect of widespread job losses. The idea that intelligent machines will eventually be able to do almost everything that humans currently do in the workplace, leading to mass unemployment and significant societal disruption, is a narrative that often comes up in discussions about AI.

This vision of a future where robots and algorithms entirely supplant human labor can be quite unsettling. It paints a picture where human skills and effort become obsolete, leading to financial hardship and a loss of purpose for many people. This fear is amplified by historical examples of technological advancements that have indeed led to shifts in the job market, where certain types of work have declined as new technologies emerged. Think about how the invention of the car changed the need for those who worked with horses and carriages. It's natural to draw parallels and wonder if AI represents a similar, but much larger, wave of technological unemployment.

However, while these concerns about automation are certainly valid and deserve careful consideration, focusing solely on this potential threat of replacement might prevent us from seeing a more complete and nuanced picture of AI's impact. By dwelling only on the idea that AI will take our jobs, we might miss out on exploring the ways in which humans and AI can actually work together, collaborating to achieve things that neither could do alone. This more optimistic perspective suggests that instead of outright replacement, AI will act as a powerful tool that enhances our own capabilities, leading to new forms of work and value creation across various fields.

Consider, for instance, the changes that technology has brought to various industries over the years. While some jobs may have been automated, new roles and opportunities have also emerged that we couldn't have imagined before. The development, implementation and maintenance of these new technologies require a skilled workforce. Think about the field of computer programming itself – it's a massive industry that exists because of the technologies that some people now fear. Similarly, the rise of AI is already creating demand for professionals in areas like AI development, data science and robotics engineering.

Furthermore, the integration of AI into existing industries isn't just about machines taking over; it's also about transforming the jobs that humans do. Instead of performing repetitive or mundane tasks, people can be freed up to focus on more complex, creative and strategic aspects of their work. Imagine a factory where robots handle repetitive assembly line tasks. This doesn't necessarily mean that all human workers are out of a job. Instead, they might transition into roles that involve programming and supervising these robots, maintaining the systems and focusing on the overall design and innovation of the production process. This shift allows humans to leverage their unique abilities in problem-solving, critical thinking and creativity, while AI handles the more routine and data-intensive work - so AI enhances what humans can do rather than simply eliminating the need for human input.

Another initial anxiety that often comes up is the fear of losing control to AI. Some people worry about a future where AI becomes so advanced that it surpasses human intelligence and begins to make decisions that are not in our best interests. This is of course probable and can lead to concerns about AI safety, wondering if we can ensure that these powerful systems operate reliably and without unintended harmful consequences. It's like thinking about building codes for houses – we need rules and safeguards in place to make sure AI is developed and used responsibly.

Related to this is the worry about AI accountability. If an AI system makes a mistake or causes harm, who is responsible? Is it the developers, the users or the AI itself? This question of "who's in charge" becomes increasingly important as AI takes on more complex and autonomous tasks. We need to establish clear lines of responsibility and ensure that there are mechanisms in place to address any negative outcomes resulting from AI actions.

Ethical considerations also play a significant role in initial anxieties about AI. One major concern is algorithmic bias. AI systems learn from the data they are trained on and if that data reflects existing societal biases, the AI can perpetuate and even amplify these unfair prejudices. Imagine an AI referee who makes unfair calls because it was trained on data that contained biased outcomes. This can lead to discriminatory outcomes in various areas, from hiring processes to loan applications. Ensuring fairness and equity in AI systems is a crucial ethical challenge that needs to be addressed proactively.

Data privacy is another key ethical concern. AI systems often require access to vast amounts of personal information to function effectively. There are worries about how this data is collected, stored and used and the potential for misuse or security breaches. It's like the idea of keeping your diary private – people want to ensure that their personal information is protected and not used without their consent or in ways that could harm them.

Beyond these immediate practical and ethical concerns, some initial anxieties about AI delve into more philosophical questions about the very nature of being human in a world increasingly populated by intelligent machines. As AI takes on tasks that were once seen as exclusive for people, it prompts us to reconsider what truly sets us apart. Questions about consciousness, creativity, empathy and our sense of self in relation to these advanced technologies naturally arise.

However, it's important to remember that our understanding of AI is still evolving and the future of its development and integration into our lives is not predetermined. By acknowledging and addressing these initial anxieties and misconceptions openly and proactively, we can move towards a more informed and balanced perspective on the role of AI in shaping our future. Instead of viewing AI solely as a threat, we can begin to see it as a powerful tool that, when developed and used responsibly, has the potential to augment human capabilities, create new opportunities and ultimately contribute to a better future for everyone. This requires a focus on ethical development, continuous learning and adaptation and a collaborative approach that involves individuals, businesses, policymakers and researchers working together to navigate this technological transformation. By understanding both the potential benefits and the risks, we can strive to harness the transformative power of AI in a way that aligns with human values and promotes a just, equitable and sustainable future.

MOVING BEYOND THE NARRATIVE OF REPLACEMENT

Instead of just thinking about the future with a sense of unease, picturing intelligent machines simply taking over and leaving us with nothing to do, perhaps we can look at it differently. The narrative that often dominates discussions around artificial intelligence focuses on the potential for machines to replace human workers, sparking understandable anxieties about job displacement and the very essence of human relevance. It's easy to get caught up in the idea of robots and algorithms stepping into our roles, automating tasks and rendering our skills obsolete.

However, what if we shifted our perspective? What if we started to see this wave of technological advancement not as a tide of replacement, but as a surge of powerful tools designed to amplify what we can already do? This is the core of a more nuanced understanding, a move beyond the simplistic narrative of machines versus humans. It's about recognizing that artificial intelligence, in its increasing capability, might actually be setting the stage for a future where technology amplifies our inherent abilities.

Imagine a scenario where instead of elimination, we see enhancement. Think about how everyday tools have always extended our physical capabilities. A hammer makes us stronger; a car makes us faster. Now, imagine tools that extend our mental capabilities. This is the essence of the augmented contribution perspective. It suggests that AI won't just take away jobs; it will serve as a potent catalyst, enabling us to become more capable, more efficient and ultimately, to generate new forms of value in countless areas of our lives and work.

Consider the world of manufacturing, for example. Instead of envisioning fully automated factories devoid of human presence, picture a collaborative environment. Repetitive or physically demanding tasks, the kind that can lead to fatigue or even injury, could be handled by intelligent robots. This doesn't mean the human workers are no longer needed. Instead, they are freed up to focus on the more intricate, creative and strategic aspects of the production process. They might be involved in designing and programming these robots, in overseeing complex operations, in problem-solving when unexpected issues arise or in driving innovation for new and better products. The human ingenuity and critical thinking remain essential, now amplified by the tireless efficiency of AI.

This transformation isn't limited to the factory floor. Think about fields like customer service. Instead of chatbots entirely replacing human agents, imagine AI systems acting as super-assistants. They could quickly access and process vast amounts of information, providing human agents with the data they need to answer complex customer queries efficiently. They could handle routine inquiries, freeing up human agents to focus on more sensitive or unique situations that require empathy and nuanced understanding. In this way, AI enhances the human agent's ability to provide better, more personalized service.

Even in creative fields, where human originality is highly valued, AI can play a role in augmentation. Imagine a writer facing writer's block. AI tools can help brainstorm ideas, suggest different phrasing or even generate initial drafts of content. The writer retains the ultimate creative control, shaping and refining the AI-generated suggestions to fit their vision. Similarly, in music composition, AI can help explore new melodies and harmonies, acting as a digital muse to inspire human composers. The core artistic intent and emotional depth still come from the human creator, but AI provides a powerful tool for exploration and experimentation.

This perspective of augmentation resonates deeply when you consider how technology has always evolved. Throughout history, new technologies have often been met with fears of job displacement. The industrial revolution brought automation that changed the landscape of work, but it also created entirely new industries and roles that we couldn't have imagined before. The advent of computers and the internet led to similar anxieties, yet they ultimately generated a massive expansion of the digital economy and new types of jobs that require out unique skills in a technologically advanced world.

The key takeaway here is that the relationship between humans and AI doesn't have to be a zero-sum game. It's not necessarily about one replacing the other. Instead, it has the potential to be a synergistic partnership, where the strengths of humans and AI complement each other. AI excels at processing vast amounts of data, identifying patterns and performing repetitive tasks with speed and accuracy. Humans bring creativity, emotional intelligence, critical thinking and the ability to adapt to novel situations. When these capabilities are combined, the potential for innovation and productivity is immense.

This shift in perspective, from replacement to augmentation, allows us to approach the future of AI with a sense of hope and opportunity rather than just fear. It encourages us to focus on identifying and cultivating the unique skills that will be even more valuable in an AI-driven world. These include things like complex problem-solving, creative thinking, emotional intelligence, communication, collaboration and critical analysis. By recognizing the enduring importance of these human attributes, we can better prepare ourselves and future generations to thrive in the age of intelligent machines.

Of course, acknowledging the potential for augmentation doesn't mean ignoring the valid concerns about automation and job displacement. It's crucial to have open and honest conversations about these challenges and to develop strategies for mitigating potential negative impacts. This might involve investing in education and training programs to help workers adapt to new roles, exploring new models of social support and ensuring that the benefits of AI are distributed broadly across society.

However, by primarily focusing on the narrative of replacement, we risk limiting our understanding of the full potential of AI and hindering our ability to proactively shape a future where technology serves to uplift and empower humanity. Embracing the era of amplified human potential encourages us to think creatively about how we can leverage

AI to solve complex problems, drive innovation, enhance human well-being and ultimately, to redefine what it means to contribute meaningfully in an increasingly intelligent world. It's about recognizing that while AI can handle many tasks, it doesn't possess the same spark of human ingenuity, the depth of human emotion or the intuitive understanding that guides our most meaningful endeavors. These are the qualities we need to nurture and value even more as we move forward in this remarkable new era.

THE AGE OF AUGMENTED CONTRIBUTION

Building upon the foundational discussions about the AI revolution and the fundamental question of what it means to be human, I want to now shift our focus towards a more optimistic and, I believe, a more accurate perspective on the future we are building with artificial intelligence.

As someone who started their career on the manufacturing floor, focused on the tangible aspects of production and then transitioned into the rapidly evolving world of technology, I've witnessed firsthand how new tools have always reshaped our work and lives. Think back to the early days of automation in automotive manufacturing. There were anxieties then too, about machines replacing human hands. But what we've seen over time is that technology has largely augmented our capabilities, allowing us to achieve more, produce higher quality goods and often, create entirely new types of jobs and industries. This is the lens through which I view the rise of AI, not as a harbinger of human obsolescence, but as the next generation of powerful tools poised to amplify our inherent human potential.

For too long, the dominant storyline has been one of replacement – robots taking our jobs, algorithms outsmarting us and humans becoming increasingly irrelevant. While it's crucial to acknowledge and address potential challenges like job displacement, I believe fixating solely on this narrative obscures the far greater potential for AI to act as a powerful catalyst for human enhancement and innovation.

Imagine a seesaw: a simple lever. It lets a child lift an adult by shifting the fulcrum. That's a lever's power – amplifying physical strength. AI acts similarly, but for the mind. Think of it as a "cognitive lever." Where a lever boosts muscle, AI boosts brainpower. Just as the seesaw makes heavy lifting easy, AI makes complex thinking easier. It takes vast data, finds patterns and offers solutions beyond human capacity. AI can enhance creativity by suggesting novel ideas, solve intricate problems by analyzing massive datasets and amplify intelligence by automating tedious tasks. It's a tool that extends our mental reach, making the seemingly impossible, achievable.

Consider a researcher sifting through mountains of data to find a crucial insight that could lead to a medical breakthrough. This is a time-consuming and often painstaking process. Now, envision that same researcher leveraging AI-powered tools that can analyze this data at lightning speed, identifying patterns and correlations that a human might miss. The AI isn't replacing the researcher's expertise or critical thinking, but it's acting as an incredibly efficient assistant, freeing up the researcher to focus on the higher-level tasks of interpreting the findings, formulating hypotheses and designing experiments. It's like having a super-powered research assistant available around the clock.

This augmentation isn't limited to scientific endeavors. Think about the creative fields. Some might fear AI will supplant artists, writers and musicians. However, I see a future where AI acts as a powerful tool for creative exploration, a powerful tool that can help generate initial ideas, explore new styles or even automate some of the more mundane aspects of content creation. A musician, facing a creative block, could use AI to experiment with different melodies and harmonies, acting as a "digital muse". The core artistic vision, the emotional depth – these still come from the human artist. The AI simply broadens their palette and accelerates the creative process. It's akin to how the invention of new musical instruments has always expanded the possibilities of musical expression.

This idea of augmented human contribution isn't just about making existing tasks easier or faster; it's about enabling entirely new forms of value creation and contribution across all domains. By taking over routine and repetitive tasks – think of AI automating mundane data entry or managing complex logistics – it frees up human capital for more strategic, creative and complex endeavors. We can shift our focus from the tactical to the strategic, from the routine to the innovative.

Consider the field of education. AI-powered personalized learning platforms can adapt to individual student needs, providing tailored lessons and feedback. This doesn't replace the vital role of the teacher, who provides mentorship, inspires critical thinking and fosters social-emotional development. Instead, AI acts as a powerful tool to personalize the learning experience, allowing teachers to focus more on individual student engagement and deeper understanding. It's like having a highly customized lesson plan that evolves in real-time based on how each student learns.

While AI can process vast amounts of data and identify patterns, it currently lacks the nuanced understanding, emotional intelligence and the ability to think truly outside the box that define human creativity. Our "gut feeling," our intuition, which is often rooted in years of experience and subconscious pattern recognition, is a trait that will continue to be vital, especially when navigating complex and uncertain situations. It's like a seasoned mechanic who can often diagnose a problem with a car just by the way it sounds, an insight that might not immediately be apparent from diagnostic data alone.

The future I envision and the one I hope this book contributes to, is one built on the synergy of human skills augmented by AI efficiency. It's about combining the strengths of both. AI excels at data processing, automation and identifying trends with speed and accuracy. Humans bring creativity, empathy, critical thinking, ethical judgment and the ability to adapt to novel situations. When these capabilities work in tandem, the potential for innovation and progress is limitless. Think back to the introduction of collaborative robots or "cobots," in manufacturing. These machines are designed to work alongside human workers, handling physically demanding or repetitive tasks, while humans oversee the process, apply their expertise and handle more complex problem-solving. This human-machine partnership leads to increased efficiency and improved quality, while also making the work environment safer and potentially more fulfilling for human workers. AI offers a similar opportunity for cognitive tasks, allowing us to offload the "heavy lifting" of data analysis and routine decision-making, freeing us to focus on what truly requires our unique human abilities.

By fostering a deeper understanding of AI's capabilities and limitations and by focusing on cultivating our skills, we can navigate this technological transformation in a way that not only preserves but also enhances what it means to be human. This idea of Collaborative Intelligence is not just a hopeful aspiration; it's a framework for understanding how we can shape a future where humans and AI work together to create a more prosperous, innovative and fulfilling world for all.

REFRAMING THE ECONOMIC AND SOCIETAL IMPACT OF AI

Building on the idea that the age we are entering is one of "Augmented Contribution," it's crucial to challenge the more common, often fear-driven narrative surrounding artificial intelligence and its effect on our economies and societies. Instead of viewing AI primarily as a force of automation that will inevitably lead to widespread job losses and societal disruption, we need to shift our perspective to recognize its potential as a powerful engine for economic growth and a tool for significant societal advancement.

Picture early 20th-century farms. Tractors arrived, replacing manual labor. Fears arose: lost jobs, disrupted livelihoods. Yet, tractors revolutionized agriculture. Food production soared, costs plummeted and new industries emerged as displaced workers found different roles. This transformation wasn't painless, but it was profoundly productive.

Now, consider AI. It's akin to the tractor, but for the mind. AI automates not just physical tasks, like intelligent machines on factory floors, but also cognitive ones, like data analysis and content creation. Just as tractors changed farming, AI will reshape numerous sectors. While job roles will inevitably shift, AI's ability to enhance efficiency, solve complex problems and generate new possibilities is immense. It's a cognitive revolution, promising to unlock productivity gains and drive innovation, just as the tractor did for agriculture, but on a broader scale. The transition will require adaptation, but the potential benefits for society are substantial.

The prevalent narrative often paints a picture of robots and algorithms stepping into our workplaces, performing tasks faster and cheaper, leaving humans with little to no role. It's easy to get caught up in this vision of widespread technological unemployment. However, this perspective often overlooks a fundamental aspect of technological progress: its capacity to create new opportunities and reshape existing ones in beneficial ways.

Let's consider another example of how technology has historically impacted the economy. The invention of the printing press, for example, didn't eliminate the need for scribes overnight, but it did democratize access to information, leading to an explosion of literacy, new forms of intellectual discourse and ultimately, the creation of entirely new professions in publishing, education and journalism.

Similarly, the rise of the internet transformed communication and commerce in ways that were hard to imagine in its early days, leading to countless new jobs and industries. AI is likely to follow a similar trajectory.

Instead of focusing solely on the jobs that might be automated, we should consider how AI can act as a catalyst for economic growth. Imagine a small business owner who previously spent countless hours on tasks like managing inventory, analyzing customer data or creating basic marketing materials. With AI-powered tools, many of these routine tasks can be automated or streamlined, freeing up the owner's time and resources to focus on more strategic activities like developing new products, exploring new markets or improving customer relationships. It's like giving that business owner a team of tireless and efficient virtual assistants, allowing their business to grow and potentially create more jobs in the long run.

Moreover, AI can drive innovation by enabling us to analyze vast amounts of data and identify patterns that would be impossible for humans to discern on their own. Think of a detective trying to solve a complex case by sifting through thousands of clues. AI can act like a super-powered assistant detective, quickly identifying connections and potential leads, allowing the human detective to focus on the critical thinking and intuitive leaps needed to crack the case. In a business context, this could lead to the development of entirely new products, services and business models that we haven't even conceived of yet. This innovation-driven growth can fuel economic expansion and create new avenues for employment.

The reframed perspective also emphasizes that AI is not just about automating existing jobs; it's about enhancing human capabilities and enabling new forms of value creation. Consider a chef in a busy restaurant. AI-powered tools could help manage inventory, predict ingredient needs and even suggest new recipes based on customer preferences and available ingredients. This doesn't replace the chef's culinary skills and creativity, but it augments their ability to run the kitchen efficiently and innovate with new dishes, potentially leading to a more successful restaurant and more jobs for kitchen staff.

Furthermore, AI can contribute to societal advancement in numerous ways beyond just economic indicators. Think about the field of healthcare. AI can assist doctors in diagnosing diseases earlier and more accurately by analyzing medical images and patient data. It can also personalize treatment plans based on an individual's specific needs and genetic makeup. It's like having a highly specialized medical consultant available to every doctor, leading to better patient outcomes and potentially a more efficient healthcare system. This can improve the quality of life for individuals and reduce the overall burden of disease on society.

In education, AI-powered personalized learning platforms can adapt to the individual learning styles and paces of students. Imagine a student struggling with a particular concept in math. An AI tutor can identify the specific areas of difficulty and provide tailored explanations and practice exercises, acting like a private tutor available 24/7. This can lead to improved learning outcomes, reduced educational disparities and a more skilled workforce in the future.

Imagine a world where everyone has equal access. That's the potential of AI for social justice. Think of it as a digital equalizer, leveling the playing field. AI can overcome barriers that traditionally exclude people. For example, AI-driven screen readers can transform online images into detailed descriptions for visually impaired users. This opens up the internet, making information and opportunities accessible. Similarly, real-time translation tools bridge language gaps, enabling seamless communication between people from different linguistic backgrounds. This is vital in healthcare, education and legal settings, ensuring everyone understands and is understood. Essentially, AI provides personalized access tools, acting as digital assistants that adapt to individual needs. It's like having an intelligent interpreter and a personal guide all rolled into one. By removing obstacles to communication and information, AI promotes inclusion and empowers individuals to participate fully in society, creating a fairer and more equitable world. It's about building a digital infrastructure where everyone belongs.

However, it's important to acknowledge that this positive reframing doesn't mean we should ignore the potential challenges. The integration of AI into our economies and societies requires careful consideration of ethical implications, data privacy and the need for continuous learning and adaptation. Just like the introduction of cars required new traffic laws and driver education, the widespread adoption of AI will necessitate new frameworks and policies to ensure its responsible and beneficial use. We need to address concerns about algorithmic bias, ensure fair access to AI technologies and invest in education and training programs to help people develop the skills needed for the evolving job market.

The key is to approach the future of AI not with a sense of passive resignation to potential job displacement, but with a proactive mindset focused on leveraging AI as a powerful tool to enhance human potential and drive positive economic and societal change. By reframing our perspective, we can move beyond the narrative of replacement and embrace the Human-AI Synergy where humans and AI work together to create a more prosperous, innovative and equitable future for all.

In essence, reframing the economic and societal impact of AI means recognizing that technological progress has historically been a force for creating new opportunities and improving lives, even as it transforms existing industries and job roles. AI, while representing a significant leap in technological capability, has the potential to follow this trend. By focusing on how AI can augment human skills, drive innovation and address societal challenges, rather than solely dwelling on the risks of automation, we can foster a more optimistic and ultimately more accurate understanding of the future we are building together with intelligent machines. This shift in perspective is crucial for guiding our strategies, investments and policies to ensure that the AI revolution leads to widespread human flourishing.

ENHANCING HUMAN CAPABILITIES WITH AI

This perspective is crucial for understanding the true potential of AI and moving away from the limiting narrative of mere automation and replacement. Just as humans have always used tools to amplify their physical strength and extend their reach, AI represents a new generation of tools designed to amplify our intellectual and creative potential.

Think back to a time when you might have used a calculator to solve a complex math problem. The calculator didn't replace our understanding of mathematics, but it certainly allowed you to perform calculations much faster and more accurately, freeing up our mental energy to focus on the broader problem-solving strategy. AI operates in a similar way, acting as a cognitive and creative partner that can extend the boundaries of what humans can achieve.

One of the most significant ways AI enhances our capabilities is by augmenting our cognitive functions. Consider something as fundamental as memory. In our daily lives, we often rely on notes, calendars and search engines to keep track of information. Now, imagine having a "digital brain" – AI-powered tools that can not only store vast amounts of information but also retrieve it instantly and organize it in a way that's most useful to you. This isn't about replacing our natural memory, but about enhancing it, allowing us to access and utilize knowledge more effectively. For example, in research, an AI could efficiently analyze millions of documents in seconds to find the exact information a human scholar needs, allowing the researcher to spend more time on analysis and interpretation, rather than tedious searching.

AI also has the potential to revolutionize personalized learning and accelerate skill development. Think of having a "private tutor" who understands your individual learning style, identifies your areas of strength and weakness and adapts the teaching methods accordingly. AI-powered educational platforms can analyze a student's performance, identify areas where they are struggling and provide tailored lessons and exercises to help them grasp concepts more effectively. This personalized approach can make learning more engaging, efficient and ultimately lead to a deeper understanding of the subject matter. Whether it's learning a new language or mastering a complex technical skill, AI can act as a patient and adaptive guide, helping individuals reach their full potential.

Furthermore, AI serves as an invaluable tool for enhancing decision-making. In today's world, we are often faced with vast amounts of data, making it difficult to identify meaningful patterns and make informed choices. AI can act as a "wise advisor" by analyzing this data at speeds and scales far beyond human capacity, providing insights and predictions that can support more informed and objective decisions. Imagine a business leader trying to understand complex market trends to inform their strategy. AI tools can quickly process sales figures, customer feedback and economic indicators to reveal hidden patterns and potential opportunities, allowing the leader to make strategic decisions with greater confidence. This ability to navigate complexity with intelligent insights is becoming increasingly crucial in a rapidly changing world.

Beyond these analytical capabilities, AI is also proving to be a powerful force in unleashing new realms of creativity and innovation. Think of AI as a "creative assistant" for artists, writers, musicians and designers. Generative AI models can learn from vast datasets of existing creative works and then generate entirely new content, from drafting a poem to composing a melody or designing a product. This doesn't diminish the role of human creativity but rather acts as a powerful tool for exploration and experimentation. For instance, a songwriter might use AI to explore different harmonic progressions or generate initial melodic ideas, which they can then refine and build upon with their own artistic vision. Similarly, a graphic designer could use AI to quickly generate a range of visual concepts based on a brief, allowing them to focus on selecting the most promising directions and adding their unique artistic flair.

The impact of AI on enhancing human capabilities extends beyond the cognitive and creative realms to the augmentation of physical tasks and sensory perception. Consider individuals with disabilities. AI-powered prosthetics are becoming increasingly sophisticated, offering more precise and intuitive control, almost like giving someone "superpowers" to overcome physical limitations. AI can also enhance sensory perception. For example, AI-powered hearing aids can filter out background noise and amplify specific sounds, improving auditory clarity. Similarly, AI-driven visual aids can provide real-time object recognition and navigation assistance for the visually impaired, acting as "enhanced senses" that expand their ability to interact with the world.

In the workplace, AI is transforming how we approach routine and repetitive tasks. Imagine a factory where robots handle the physically demanding and monotonous assembly line work. This doesn't necessarily mean fewer jobs for humans but rather a shift in roles. Humans can then focus on more complex, creative and strategic aspects of the manufacturing process, such as designing new products, programming and maintaining the robots and ensuring quality control. This is the essence of AI augmentation as cooperation – humans and AI working in tandem, each contributing their unique strengths. AI handles the tasks that are often tedious and error-prone for humans, freeing up our time and energy for work that requires critical thinking, problem-solving and ingenuity.

Furthermore, AI is playing a significant role in improving communication and collaboration. Think of AI-powered language translation tools as a "global communication catalyst" instantly breaking down language barriers and enabling seamless communication between people from different cultures. This facilitates global collaboration and understanding in various fields, from business to scientific research to personal relationships. AI can also enhance interpersonal interactions by analyzing communication patterns and providing feedback, potentially leading to more effective and empathetic communication.

Ultimately, AI as a powerful tool for enhancing human capabilities is about synergy. It's not about humans versus machines, but about humans *with* machines. AI excels at processing vast amounts of data, identifying patterns and performing repetitive tasks with speed and accuracy. Humans bring creativity, emotional intelligence, critical thinking and the ability to adapt to novel situations. When these strengths are combined, the potential for innovation, productivity and overall human flourishing is immense. Just like a team of skilled craftspeople using specialized tools to create something extraordinary, humans and AI working together can achieve results that were previously unimaginable.

This perspective moves us beyond the anxieties of job displacement and towards a future where technology empowers us to be more capable, more creative and more effective in all aspects of our lives. Embracing this understanding of AI as a tool for augmentation is key to navigating the future with optimism and harnessing its transformative power for the betterment of humanity. Our next step should be to think about the specific ways this augmentation is impacting different industries and sectors, providing concrete examples of this powerful synergy in action.

ENABLING NEW FORMS OF VALUE CREATION

Next focusing on the empowering aspect of artificial intelligence. As we establish, the Symbiotic Intelligence Era that center on the idea that AI is not simply about taking over tasks but about making us, as humans, more capable across various facets of life. Let's explore in detail how AI acts as this powerful enhancer of our abilities.

One of the most profound ways AI serves as an amplifier is in the realm of our cognitive abilities. Our minds are incredibly powerful, but they have natural limitations in terms of processing speed, memory capacity and the ability to discern patterns within massive datasets. AI excels in these areas, acting like a significant upgrade to our inherent mental capabilities.

Consider the act of remembering information. While humans have sophisticated memory systems, recalling specific details from a vast amount of data can be time-consuming and sometimes unreliable. AI-powered tools can step in as a form of enhanced memory, acting like a perfectly organized and instantly accessible digital archive. Imagine trying to recall a specific piece of information from years of research or countless documents. AI can navigate this ocean of data in mere moments, retrieving exactly what you need, allowing you to focus your mental energy on analysis, interpretation and drawing new connections. This isn't about our brains becoming lazy; it's about freeing them from the burden of rote memorization to engage in higher-level thinking. Think of it like having a perfectly organized filing system for your mind, managed by an incredibly efficient assistant.

Furthermore, AI is transforming the landscape of learning and skill development through personalized experiences. We all learn at different paces and have unique learning styles. Traditional educational methods often adopt a one-size-fits-all approach, which can leave some learners behind while not fully challenging others. AI, however, can act as a highly adaptive "private tutor" which is also briefly mentioned before in the book. Imagine a learning platform that adjusts its teaching methods and the difficulty of the material based on your individual progress and understanding. If you're struggling with a particular concept, the AI can provide additional explanations, examples or alternative approaches until you grasp it. If you're excelling, it can introduce more advanced topics to keep you engaged and challenged. This tailored approach can dramatically accelerate the learning process and ensure a deeper, more personalized understanding, helping everyone reach their full potential in acquiring new knowledge and skills.

The ability to make informed decisions is fundamental in both our personal and professional lives. However, navigating complex situations with numerous variables and vast amounts of information can be overwhelming. This is where AI steps in as an invaluable "wise advisor". By analyzing large datasets and identifying subtle patterns that might be invisible to the human eye, AI can provide insights and predictions that significantly enhance our decision-making capabilities. Consider trying to understand trends in a complex market. AI can process data on consumer behavior, economic indicators and competitor activities to reveal emerging opportunities or potential risks, allowing leaders to make more strategic and data-driven choices. This isn't about AI making the decisions for us, but about providing us with the clarity and insights needed to make better, more confident choices. It's like having an incredibly astute analyst who can quickly synthesize complex information and present you with clear, actionable intelligence.

Beyond these logical and analytical enhancements, AI is also proving to be a powerful catalyst for creativity and innovation. While the spark of human imagination remains essential, AI can act as a tool for creative generation by helping us explore new ideas and generate novel content across various domains. Imagine a writer facing a blank page. AI tools can offer suggestions for plotlines, different phrasing or even generate initial drafts, acting as a brainstorming partner to overcome creative blocks. Similarly, in music, AI can be used to experiment with different melodies, harmonies and rhythms, providing a "musical partner" for composers to explore new sonic landscapes. In design, AI can rapidly generate a multitude of visual concepts based on specific requirements, allowing designers to focus on refining the most promising ideas and adding their unique artistic vision. This collaboration between human creativity and AI's generative power can lead to breakthroughs and innovations that might not have been possible otherwise.

The transformative power of AI also extends to the physical realm through the augmentation of tasks and sensory experiences. For individuals facing physical limitations, AI-powered prosthetics and assistive devices can offer increased mobility, dexterity and independence. Imagine prosthetic limbs controlled by neural interfaces that allow for more natural and precise movements, effectively giving individuals 'superpowers' to overcome physical challenges. Furthermore, AI can enhance our natural senses. Instead of AI screen readers, consider AI-powered exoskeletons designed for rehabilitation and mobility. These devices use machine learning to adapt to the user's movements, assisting individuals with paralysis or muscle weakness to walk, climb stairs and perform daily tasks. By analyzing the user's intended movements and providing precise support, these exoskeletons can significantly improve quality of life and promote physical independence. Similarly, AI-driven visual aids can analyze the environment and provide real-time information to visually impaired individuals, augmenting their perception of the world.

In the workplace, AI is revolutionizing how we handle routine and repetitive tasks. Imagine factory workers being freed from physically demanding and monotonous assembly line duties by collaborative robots that work alongside them. This "AI augmentation as cooperation" allows humans to focus on more complex, creative and strategic aspects of their work, such as problem-solving, quality control and innovation. By taking over tasks that are often error-prone and draining for humans, AI can lead to increased efficiency, improved safety and ultimately, higher quality outcomes.

Finally, AI is playing an increasingly important role in improving communication and fostering collaboration across various divides. Imagine language translation tools that can instantly bridge communication gaps, acting as a language interpretation platform and enabling people from different linguistic backgrounds to understand each other seamlessly. AI can also analyze communication patterns within teams, providing feedback that can lead to more effective and empathetic interactions. This enhanced communication and collaboration, facilitated by AI, can lead to more inclusive environments, stronger relationships and better outcomes in both personal and professional settings.

In essence, AI as a powerful tool for enhancing human capabilities is about creating a symbiotic relationship where the strengths of both humans and AI are leveraged to achieve more than either could accomplish alone. It's about moving beyond the fear of replacement and embracing a future where technology empowers us to be more intelligent, more creative, more capable and more connected. This understanding forms the bedrock of the flourishing of Human Capability, a positive framework for navigating the future of AI with hope and a focus on amplifying human potential. Our next logical step is to explore how this augmentation is specifically playing out across different industries and sectors, bringing this powerful concept to life with concrete examples of its transformative impact.

HUMAN INGENUITY, CREATIVITY AND CRITICAL THINKING

Bringing up the concept of Intelligent Partnership, it becomes clear that AI, for all its remarkable capabilities, acts as a powerful amplifier of our inherent human strengths. Let's explore these vital human attributes in detail.

Ingenuity, at its core, is the ability to come up with original, clever and often unexpected ideas or solutions to problems. It's about thinking beyond the existing frameworks, connecting seemingly disparate concepts and envisioning possibilities that were previously unseen. This uniquely human capacity is driven by our curiosity, our ability to make intuitive leaps and our intrinsic desire to understand and shape the world around us.

While AI can process vast amounts of information and identify patterns that might elude human observation, it operates within the boundaries of the data it has been trained on and the algorithms that guide it. It can generate novel outputs, but these are ultimately derived from existing knowledge and patterns. True ingenuity, on the other hand, often involves breaking free from established patterns and conceiving of something truly new.

Consider the invention of the wheel. There was no pre-existing data or algorithm that could have directly led to this groundbreaking innovation. It required a flash of insight, a novel way of thinking about movement and load-bearing, driven by a human need to overcome limitations. Similarly, the concept of the internet wasn't a logical extrapolation of existing communication technologies alone; it required a visionary leap in imagining a globally interconnected network. These acts of ingenuity are characterized by a spark of original thought, a "lightbulb moment" that stems from human curiosity and the ability to make abstract connections.

Think of it like a bird building a nest. While a bird follows its instincts and uses available materials, the specific design and adaptation of the nest to its environment and needs can be seen as a form of natural ingenuity. It's a creative solution to a fundamental problem – shelter and safety for its young. Human ingenuity operates on a similar principle but with a far greater capacity for abstract thought and complex problem-solving.

AI can be a powerful tool in the *execution* of ingenious ideas, helping us to model, test and refine them with unprecedented speed and efficiency. However, the initial spark of truly novel thought, the ability to envision a completely new approach or a revolutionary solution, remains firmly within the realm of human ingenuity. For example, AI might help engineers optimize the design of a new type of engine, but the initial ingenious concept for that engine likely originated from a human mind grappling with the fundamental principles of physics and the need for more efficient power.

Creativity is the ability to generate new and valuable ideas, make connections between seemingly unrelated concepts and express oneself in novel and meaningful ways. It involves imagination originality and the capacity to produce something that is both new and has value or resonance.

While Generative AI has demonstrated a remarkable ability to produce original content, such as text, images, music and code, it's crucial to understand the fundamental differences between AI-generated content and human creativity. AI's creations are based on patterns learned from vast datasets of existing human-created content. It excels at imitation, recombination and even the generation of statistically novel outputs. However, it currently lacks the intrinsic motivation, emotional depth and subjective experiences that often drive human creative expression.

Consider AI-generated art as digital finger painting. It can produce visually interesting and even aesthetically pleasing results based on learned styles and patterns. However, the art created by a human often stems from a personal vision, an emotional response to the world or a desire to communicate a specific feeling or idea. Think of an artist who pours their grief or joy onto a canvas – the resulting artwork carries an emotional weight and a personal narrative that is fundamentally different from AI-generated imagery.

Similarly, in music, AI can compose intricate melodies and harmonies in various styles. Imagine an AI composing music like a digital orchestra, capable of playing various tunes. However, music created by a human composer often reflects their lived experiences, their cultural influences and their emotional landscape. A song written about love or loss carries a depth of feeling that is rooted in human consciousness and empathy.

Human creativity is also crucial for problem-solving in novel and ambiguous situations. When faced with unprecedented challenges, humans can draw upon their imagination, intuition and ability to think "outside the box" to devise innovative solutions. AI, while powerful in analyzing existing data and optimizing known processes, may struggle to generate truly creative solutions when confronted with entirely new scenarios that lack historical precedent in its training data. This ability to approach problems with fresh perspectives and imaginative thinking is what drives breakthroughs in science, technology and all other fields of human endeavor.

Critical thinking is the ability to analyze information objectively, evaluate arguments, identify biases and form reasoned judgments. It involves logic, reasoning and the ability to consider different perspectives and make informed decisions based on evidence and sound judgment.

AI excels at processing vast amounts of data and identifying correlations. It can rapidly analyze information and provide insights that can inform human decision-making. However, true critical thinking goes beyond mere data processing. It requires the ability to understand context, to make nuanced judgments, to consider ethical implications and to apply common sense and real-world knowledge.

Imagine AI as following traffic directions. It can efficiently guide you from point A to point B based on the provided data (maps, traffic conditions). However, if there's an unexpected road closure or a detour that isn't yet reflected in the data, a human driver needs to exercise critical thinking to assess the situation, consider alternative routes and make a reasoned decision about how to proceed. AI, in such a situation, might simply indicate that the planned route is unavailable without the ability to creatively problem-solve the unexpected obstacle.

Furthermore, critical thinking involves the ability to evaluate the credibility and reliability of information, especially in an age where misinformation can spread rapidly. Humans can use their reasoning skills, background knowledge and ability to discern bias to assess the validity of sources and arguments. While AI can be used to detect potentially false information based on patterns, it may struggle with nuanced forms of deception or propaganda that rely on emotional manipulation or subtle misrepresentations of context.

In fields like medicine, AI might diagnose based on symptoms, identifying potential illnesses based on patterns in patient data. However, a human doctor uses critical thinking to consider the patient's individual history, lifestyle, emotional state and other contextual factors to arrive at a comprehensive diagnosis and treatment plan. This involves not just analyzing data but also exercising judgment, empathy and a deep understanding of the complexities of human health.

Ethical decision-making is another area where human critical thinking remains paramount. AI operates based on the ethical guidelines programmed into it, which are ultimately created by humans. However, navigating complex ethical dilemmas often requires considering competing values, understanding the potential consequences of different actions and making judgments based on a sense of morality and fairness that is deeply rooted in human experience and social understanding.

It's crucial to reiterate that the future isn't about humans versus AI, but rather about the powerful synergy that can be created when we combine the strengths of both. AI can augment our ingenuity by providing us with powerful tools for exploration and analysis. It can fuel our creativity by acting as a brainstorming partner and generating novel starting points. And it can enhance our critical thinking by providing us with vast amounts of data and identifying patterns that can inform our judgments.

However, the initial spark of ingenuity, the emotional depth of true creativity and the nuanced judgment of critical thinking remain human specific. Our ability to dream, to imagine, to empathize and to grapple with complex ethical considerations are what truly set us apart and will continue to be indispensable in shaping a future where technology serves humanity in meaningful ways.

While AI's capabilities continue to expand at an unprecedented rate, basic human traits remain the cornerstones of progress, innovation and meaningful human experience. As we navigate the partnership with AI, it is more important than ever to cultivate and value these traits. By embracing AI as a powerful tool that amplifies our inherent abilities, rather than viewing it as a replacement for our core human essence, we can ensure a future where human potential is not only preserved but also dramatically enhanced, leading to unprecedented levels of innovation, understanding and human flourishing. Our next step will be to dive into the practical applications of this augmented contribution across various industries, demonstrating how this synergy between human skills and AI efficiency is transforming the world of work and beyond.

THE SYNERGY OF HUMAN SKILLS AUGMENTED BY AI

It's time to further explore a central tenet of our discussion: the powerful synergy that arises from the combination of inherent human skills and the ever-increasing efficiency of artificial intelligence. This collaboration isn't a competition, but rather a dynamic partnership that unlocks potential far exceeding what either humans or AI could achieve in isolation. As we continue to build the narrative of the "Human Empowerment through AI" understanding this synergy is paramount to envisioning a thriving future. The remarkable progress in AI, particularly in generative models and large language models (LLMs), presents an opportunity to reshape work and society in profound ways, provided we embrace a nuanced understanding of this emerging collaboration and move beyond narratives of technological supremacy.

The current landscape of AI is marked by an extraordinary pace of innovation. The year 2024 witnessed significant strides in generative AI, with the emergence and refinement of several powerful models. Gemini, the multimodal LLM - including text, code, audio, images and video, unlike its primarily text-based predecessors is integrated with almost all of Google's customer facing products like Cloud, Workspace etc. Microsoft's Copilot, along with Copilot+ PCs, introduced enhanced security features and advanced data analysis capabilities within familiar applications like Excel and OneDrive. Claude AI, developed by Anthropic, distinguished itself through its capacity to process extensive and complex documents, making it particularly useful for tasks such as summarizing technical reports. These advancements signify a clear trend towards AI systems that are not only more intelligent but also more versatile and integrated into everyday workflows. The increasing integration of AI into enterprise software means that businesses across various sectors are gaining easier access to these powerful tools, enabling employees to leverage AI in their routine tasks without requiring specialized AI expertise.

Furthermore, the development of multimodal AI, capable of processing information from multiple sources like images, text and videos concurrently, is dramatically expanding the potential applications of this technology 2. This capability allows AI to interact with and understand the world in a more comprehensive manner. For instance, in educational settings, multimodal AI can facilitate more engaging and interactive learning experiences. In the retail industry, it can analyze a wider range of customer touchpoints to deliver more personalized service. Alongside these developments, the emergence of "frontier models" with advanced reasoning capabilities, such as OpenAI's o1, demonstrates the progress in creating AI that can solve complex problems using logical steps similar to human thought processes. Simultaneously, there is a growing trend towards the creation of more specialized AI models tailored for specific industries or tasks, indicating a nuanced approach to leveraging AI's potential. The development of AI agents capable of handling tasks autonomously, such as managing inventory in manufacturing or resolving IT issues in an office environment, represents another significant leap forward. These agents can proactively assist humans, taking on responsibilities and freeing up human time for more strategic endeavors.

At the core of this AI revolution are large language models (LLMs), which possess a remarkable ability to understand and generate natural language. Their functionalities extend to content creation, allowing businesses to generate high-quality blog posts, marketing materials and product descriptions at an unprecedented pace. LLMs excel at summarizing lengthy articles, translating languages with increasing accuracy, answering a wide range of questions and even assisting in the generation of computer code. Moreover, these models are increasingly adept at understanding the nuances of human communication, capable of inferring meaning from context and even detecting the sentiment behind text. The rapid evolution of these AI capabilities signifies a transformative shift, promising to enhance efficiency and productivity across numerous industries by automating repetitive tasks and providing powerful analytical tools.

Despite the remarkable efficiency and rapidly expanding capabilities of AI, certain fundamental human skills remain indispensable in this evolving landscape. While AI excels at processing data and automating tasks, the essence of human contribution lies in qualities that AI currently cannot fully replicate. Creativity, the ability to generate novel and valuable ideas, remains a uniquely human trait. While AI can assist in the creative process by generating ideas or refining existing ones, the spark of true innovation, often rooted in human intuition, emotion and a deep understanding of context, originates from human minds. AI can act as a catalyst for creativity, but it cannot replace the human artist, designer or innovator.

Critical thinking and complex problem-solving are other crucial human skills that are even more vital in the age of AI. The ability to analyze information objectively, evaluate evidence, question assumptions and form reasoned judgments is essential when interacting with AI-generated content and insights. Humans are needed to define the right problems, interpret the outputs of AI systems and make nuanced decisions based on a multitude of factors that AI may not fully comprehend. Emotional intelligence (EQ), encompassing empathy, self-awareness, social awareness and relationship management, is another domain where humans retain a distinct advantage. These skills are crucial for effective communication, collaboration, building trust and navigating the complexities of human interactions, all of which are essential in any professional or social setting. Emotionally intelligent leaders are also vital for ensuring the ethical development and deployment of AI technologies, fostering trust in these systems among users and the wider public.

Furthermore, the rapid pace of technological change, driven in large part by AI advancements, necessitates adaptability and a commitment to lifelong learning. Individuals need to continuously acquire new skills and knowledge to remain relevant in an evolving job market. Interestingly, AI itself can play a significant role in facilitating this lifelong learning process by providing personalized learning platforms and tailored upskilling opportunities. This creates a synergistic relationship where AI not only drives change but also helps humans adapt to that change. The enduring value of these human skills lies in their ability to complement the efficiency of AI, creating a powerful partnership that transcends the limitations of either entity working in isolation.

The synergy between human skills and AI efficiency is already manifesting across various industries, demonstrating the transformative potential of this collaboration. In healthcare, AI is proving to be an invaluable tool for augmenting the capabilities of medical professionals. AI algorithms can analyze medical images with remarkable speed and accuracy, assisting in the early detection of diseases and allowing doctors to focus more on patient care and treatment planning. Virtual health assistants powered by AI are streamlining routine administrative tasks, such as scheduling appointments and answering common patient inquiries, freeing up healthcare professionals to concentrate on more complex cases requiring human empathy and expertise. Moreover, AI is accelerating the process of drug discovery and enabling the development of personalized treatment plans tailored to individual patient needs, guided by the knowledge and insights of medical researchers and clinicians.

In the financial sector, AI is enhancing security and efficiency by detecting fraudulent transactions and managing financial risks. This allows human financial analysts to dedicate their time to strategic decision-making and building strong relationships with clients. AI-powered chatbots are providing round-the-clock customer service for routine inquiries, while human agents handle more complex or sensitive issues that require a nuanced understanding and emotional intelligence. Furthermore, AI is assisting in the delivery of personalized financial advice and wealth management services, making expert guidance more accessible to a wider range of individuals, all under the oversight of human financial advisors who ensure responsible and ethical practices.

The manufacturing industry is also experiencing a significant transformation through the integration of AI. AI is optimizing supply chains, predicting potential equipment maintenance needs and ensuring stringent quality control throughout the production process. Collaborative robots or cobots, are working alongside human operators on assembly lines, combining the precision and efficiency of AI with human dexterity and problem-solving abilities. This human-robot collaboration is leading to increased productivity, reduced waste and safer working conditions.

Even in the traditionally human-centric creative industries, AI is emerging as a powerful collaborative tool. AI tools are assisting artists in generating initial ideas, creating stunning visual art, composing unique musical pieces and even writing initial drafts of content. However, human artists retain ultimate creative control and inject the essential emotional depth and artistic vision that AI currently lacks. AI is also streamlining various post-production tasks in film and television, allowing human creative teams to focus on the core aspects of storytelling and artistic direction.

In the field of education, AI is facilitating more personalized and effective learning experiences. AI-powered learning platforms are adapting to the individual needs and paces of students, while teachers provide essential guidance, support and foster the development of critical thinking skills. AI tools are also automating time-consuming tasks such as grading assignments and managing administrative duties, freeing up educators to spend more quality time interacting with their students and addressing their individual learning requirements.

While the potential benefits of human-AI synergy are substantial, it is important to acknowledge the legitimate anxieties surrounding the increasing role of AI in our lives. Concerns about job displacement and the ethical implications of AI are prevalent in public discourse. However, a growing body of evidence suggests that AI is more likely to augment human capabilities and transform the nature of work rather than lead to widespread job elimination. By automating mundane and repetitive tasks, AI can free up human workers to focus on more strategic, creative and fulfilling activities. Addressing the ethical considerations surrounding AI development and deployment is paramount for fostering trust and ensuring responsible innovation. This includes mitigating biases in AI algorithms, ensuring transparency in how AI systems make decisions and establishing clear lines of accountability for AI actions. Maintaining human oversight and agency in AI-driven processes is also crucial 1 Humans should remain in control of AI systems, making final decisions and taking responsibility for the outcomes. Furthermore, promoting transparency and explainability in AI systems is essential for building confidence and trust among users and the public. Understanding how AI arrives at its conclusions is vital for ensuring its reliability and fostering its widespread adoption.

Cultivating a future where human skills and AI efficiency work in harmony requires a proactive approach from individuals, organizations and governments. The future of work is undoubtedly shifting towards roles that leverage uniquely human skills in collaboration with AI technologies. To adapt to these changes and thrive in this evolving landscape, individuals and organizations must prioritize lifelong learning and continuous upskilling. This includes not only acquiring new technical skills related to AI but also further developing uniquely human capabilities such as creativity, critical thinking and emotional intelligence. The emergence of new hybrid roles that require a blend of human skills and AI expertise underscores this evolving nature of work. As AI takes over more routine tasks, individuals will have the opportunity to focus on higher-level, more meaningful activities, potentially leading to greater job satisfaction and a more engaged workforce.

This synergistic relationship between human skills and AI efficiency offers numerous benefits:

• Increased Productivity and Efficiency: By automating routine tasks and augmenting human capabilities, the combined power of humans and AI leads to significant gains in productivity and efficiency across various industries.

• Enhanced Creativity and Innovation: AI can act as a catalyst for human creativity by providing new perspectives, generating novel ideas and freeing up human minds to focus on higher-level conceptualization and innovation.

• Improved Decision-Making: The combination of AI's data analysis capabilities with human critical thinking and contextual understanding leads to more informed, nuanced and effective decision-making.

• Greater Job Satisfaction: By automating mundane and repetitive tasks, AI can free up human workers to focus on more engaging, creative and strategic work, potentially leading to greater job satisfaction and a more fulfilling human experience.

To fully realize the potential of this synergy, several key factors are important:

• Investing in Education and Training: Preparing the workforce for the age of AI requires investing in education and training programs that focus on developing skills, such as creativity, critical thinking and emotional intelligence, as well as providing opportunities to learn how to effectively collaborate with AI tools.

• Developing Ethical Frameworks: As AI becomes more integrated into our lives and workplaces, it is crucial to develop ethical guidelines that address concerns related to bias, fairness, transparency and accountability in AI systems.

• Designing Human-Centered AI Tools: AI systems should be designed with a focus on augmenting human capabilities and enhancing the human experience, rather than simply replacing human workers. User-friendly interfaces and intuitive interactions are essential for fostering effective collaboration.

As we continue our journey into the age of intelligent machines, it is this harmonious blend of human ingenuity, creativity, critical thinking and emotional intelligence with AI's speed, precision and analytical power that will pave the way for a truly flourishing future for humanity. Our next exploration will delve into how AI is democratizing access to various human traits, further expanding potential and raising important societal considerations.

EMBRACING FUTURE - TECHNOLOGY AS A HUMAN AMPLIFIER

This perspective is rooted in the understanding that just as past technological advancements have enhanced our physical abilities, AI represents the next stage, focusing on augmenting our cognitive strengths. Instead of viewing AI as a looming force of automation destined to render human skills obsolete. This framework envisions a collaborative future where humans and AI work in synergy, achieving outcomes far greater than either could accomplish independently. As the last section of the chapter, let's revisit some of the main topics discussed in this chapter.

At its core, this endeavor involves a significant reframing of the economic and societal impact of AI. The common anxiety we discussed earlier in the book - centers on job displacement, with fears that machines will simply take over human roles. However, AI should be seen primarily as a catalyst for economic growth and societal advancement, fostering collaboration rather than substitution. Think of it like the introduction of the personal computer and the internet. Initially, there were fears of widespread job losses as computers automated tasks previously done by humans. However, the PC and internet revolutionized communication, commerce and information access. While some roles became obsolete, entirely new industries emerged, like software development, web design, e-commerce and digital marketing. These technologies didn't simply replace jobs; they created a vastly expanded digital economy, generating countless new opportunities and transforming how we live and work. Similarly, AI has the potential to reshape industries and create entirely new fields we can't even imagine yet.

This reframing directly supports the understanding of AI as a powerful tool for enhancing human capabilities. AI's ability to process and analyze vast datasets at incredible speeds, identifying patterns and insights invisible to the human eye, doesn't diminish our significance. Instead, it acts as an exceptionally intelligent assistant, providing a level of information and analysis that empowers us to make more informed decisions and be more effective in our respective domains. Consider trying to understand intricate market trends to guide a business strategy. Without AI, this would require countless hours of manual data collection and analysis. With AI, however, those insights can be obtained much faster, allowing human strategists to focus on the aspects of creative problem-solving and nuanced decision-making. It's akin to having a super-efficient research team that quickly gathers and synthesizes information, freeing up your time for higher-level strategic thought.

This enhancement of our inherent abilities naturally leads to enabling new forms of value creation and contribution across domains. When AI takes over routine and repetitive tasks, it liberates human capital to concentrate on more complex, creative and strategic endeavors. This isn't merely about performing the same tasks faster; it's about unlocking opportunities for entirely new types of work and innovation that are currently beyond our conception. Imagine a world where AI handles the laborious and time-consuming aspects of scientific research, allowing human scientists to dedicate more time to formulating groundbreaking hypotheses and designing innovative experiments. This synergy can accelerate the pace of discovery and lead to breakthroughs that were previously unattainable.

Throughout this transformative process, we need to remember that human ingenuity, creativity and critical thinking remain indispensable. While AI is a potent tool, it lacks the consciousness, empathy and nuanced critical thinking that define our humanity. These are the very qualities that enable us to adapt to novel situations, make ethical judgments and build meaningful relationships. In a world increasingly populated by intelligent machines, these human-centered skills will become even more valuable. Think of an artist using AI to generate various visual patterns. The AI can produce countless options, but it's the artist's unique vision, emotional expression and critical judgment that determine which patterns resonate and become part of a meaningful artwork. AI can be a digital brush, but the artistry lies in the human hand guiding it.

This naturally leads to the concept of the synergy of human skills augmented by AI efficiency which implies a collaboration *with* machines. AI excels at processing data and performing repetitive tasks with speed and accuracy. Humans bring creativity, emotional intelligence, critical thinking and the ability to understand context. When these distinct strengths are combined, the potential for innovation and productivity becomes immense. Consider the advancements in manufacturing with collaborative robots or "cobots". These robots can handle the physically demanding or repetitive tasks on an assembly line, freeing up human operators to focus on more intricate assembly, problem-solving and quality control. This synergy results in safer, more efficient and ultimately, higher-quality output. It's like a skilled craftsman working alongside a powerful automated tool, each contributing their unique strengths to create a superior product.

Ultimately, the way is to foster a mindset that embraces a future where technology amplifies human potential. It's about moving beyond the understandable fear of replacement and seizing the incredible opportunity for augmentation. It's about recognizing AI as a powerful partner and tool that can help us achieve more and focus on what truly makes life meaningful. This Intelligence Augmentation isn't just a hopeful aspiration; it's a pragmatic framework for understanding how we can navigate this technological transformation in a way that not only preserves but also elevates our humanity. As we move forward, it will be crucial to consider not only the *capabilities* of AI but also its cost-effectiveness and environmental impact, as well as its influence on team morale in this evolving landscape, ensuring that progress is both sustainable and beneficial for all. Just as we consider the energy efficiency of a new machine on the factory floor, we must evaluate the broader impact of AI technologies.

The journey into the age of intelligent machines is simultaneously a journey of self-discovery, prompting us to appreciate the enduring value of our consciousness, creativity, empathy and nuanced critical thinking. By embracing this perspective of augmentation and focusing on the unique strengths that define us, we can shape a future where AI serves as a catalyst for amplified human flourishing. It's about harnessing the power of technology to build a more efficient, productive, just and equitable world, driven by conscious and collaborative effort.

DEFINING HUMANITY NOW

In our ongoing exploration of this new era shaped by artificial intelligence, we now turn to a question that has echoed through the corridors of time: What truly defines humanity? As intelligent machines become more adept at tasks that once seemed exclusively human, this inquiry takes on a renewed and profound significance.

For millennia, humans have pondered the essence of their existence. Across diverse cultures and throughout history, we have strived to understand what sets us apart, what binds us together and what it truly means to be human. Ancient wisdom traditions offer foundational perspectives, often emphasizing qualities like reason, virtue, interconnectedness and self-awareness as central to the human experience. These diverse viewpoints highlight the multifaceted nature of our being, suggesting that there isn't a single, simple answer to what makes us.

Throughout history, philosophical thought has grappled with this question in profound ways. Existentialism explores the freedom and responsibility inherent in our existence, emphasizing the choices we make that define who we are. Humanism champions human agency and our potential for good, placing humanity at the center of ethical consideration. These abstract ideas resonate in our everyday lives, influencing our values, our relationships and our search for purpose. The shared human condition, encompassing the spectrum of joy and sorrow, love and loss and ultimately, mortality, further binds us together. These universal experiences contribute to our collective understanding of what it means to be alive. This inherent drive to define our existence suggests a fundamental human need for meaning-making, a need that is brought into sharp focus by the emergence of artificial intelligence. The diverse perspectives offered by philosophy underscore the complexity of this question, a complexity that becomes even more apparent when considering the rise of AI.

One of the fundamental aspects of our humanity lies in our biological makeup. Our physical form, shaped by millennia of evolution, grants us unique capabilities. Our ability to walk upright, the dexterity of our hands and the intricate complexity of our brains have enabled us to interact with the world and develop sophisticated tools and societies. Beyond our physical form, our rich sensory experiences – the way we perceive colors, sounds, textures, tastes and smells – profoundly shape our understanding of the world around us. This subjective, qualitative experience stands in contrast to the data-driven perception of AI, which processes information through sensors and algorithms. The very mystery of human consciousness, encompassing our self-awareness, our subjective experiences and our sentience – the feeling of being alive and aware – adds another profound layer to our biological blueprint. While we can draw analogies to understand complex systems in nature, such as the intricate organization of an ant colony, these comparisons often highlight the current limitations of AI in replicating the deeply personal and subjective nature of human consciousness. Our biological evolution has not only shaped our physical abilities but also the very nature of our intelligence and consciousness, a development distinct from the engineered intelligence of AI.

Humans are also fundamentally social beings. Our survival and well-being are deeply intertwined with our connections to others. The importance of family, community and social structures is evident across all cultures and throughout history. Our capacity for empathy, the ability to understand and share the feelings of others, plays a crucial role in building and maintaining these vital social connections. While AI can be programmed to recognize and respond to emotional cues, replicating the genuine understanding and shared experience of empathy remains a significant challenge. Human communication, with its intricate interplay of spoken words, body language and emotional expression, stands in contrast to the more direct and transactional communication of current AI systems. The subtle nuances of human interaction, often relying on unspoken understanding and shared context, underscore the depth of our social nature. Our ability to cooperate, to build trust and to form complex social bonds is a defining characteristic of our species.

Furthermore, our cognitive abilities are central to what we consider human. This encompasses our capacity for problem-solving, reasoning, learning and memory. While AI excels at processing vast amounts of data and identifying complex patterns, human intelligence is often characterized by its flexibility, adaptability and the ability to make intuitive leaps. Creativity, that spark of imagination, innovation and artistic expression, further distinguishes us. Think of a musician composing a new melody or an architect envisioning a unique building design. While AI can assist in generating musical variations or suggesting structural elements, the initial creative spark, the emotional intent and the overarching artistic vision typically originate from human ingenuity. Our capacity for abstract thought, enabling us to form concepts, use symbols and engage in philosophical reasoning, allows us to understand intricate ideas and build complex systems of knowledge. While AI can manipulate symbols and process abstract concepts, the human ability to generate entirely new abstractions and engage in profound philosophical inquiry remains a defining characteristic.

Finally, our emotional landscape contributes significantly to our human essence. The wide spectrum of emotions we experience, from joy and love to sorrow and fear, shapes our perceptions, drives our actions and plays a crucial role in our decision-making processes and relationships. These emotions are often not purely logical, yet they provide valuable information about our internal state and the world around us. Consider how fear might prompt us to avoid danger or how joy might strengthen our bonds with loved ones. This intricate interplay between emotions and reason in human thought and behavior is a defining characteristic. Creating AI with genuine emotional intelligence, capable of truly understanding and experiencing the richness and complexity of human emotions, remains a formidable challenge.

In the age of intelligent machines, exploring these facets of our being helps us to identify the attributes that currently distinguish humans from even the most advanced AI systems.

Qualities like consciousness, that inner awareness and subjective experience, remain a key differentiator. Creativity, driven by intention and emotional resonance, sets us apart from AI's generative capabilities. Empathy, the capacity for genuine understanding and sharing of feelings, is a fundamental aspect of human connection that AI has yet to replicate. And nuanced critical thinking, which goes beyond pure logic and data analysis, often drawing upon intuition and a wealth of lived experience, remains a distinct human strength.

The increasing interaction with AI might paradoxically lead to a renewed appreciation and focus on these human qualities. As machines take over more routine and analytical tasks, we may find ourselves with more time and space to cultivate our creativity, empathy and critical thinking skills. This shift could lead to a re-evaluation of what aspects of work and life are most meaningful and inherently human. The integration of AI has the potential to liberate us from mundane tasks, allowing us to concentrate on activities that require imagination, emotional intelligence and complex problem-solving – areas where our capabilities remain distinctly advantageous.

THE TIMELESS QUESTION

As AI gets smarter, what makes us different from machines? This is a question that has been pondered for centuries, long before the emergence of the intelligent machines we're seeing today. But now, as AI becomes increasingly capable, understanding the essence of our own humanity takes on a new and vital significance. It's like we're standing at a crossroads, needing to understand ourselves better as we navigate a world increasingly shaped by these new forms of intelligence.

At the most basic level, what makes us human starts with our physical being. Think about how we stand upright, walk on two legs and use our hands with incredible dexterity. It's like a monkey's hands, perfectly designed for grasping and manipulating things, but our hands can do even more intricate tasks. Then there are our senses – the vibrant colors we see, the melodies we hear, the textures we feel, the tastes we savor and the scents that evoke memories. Our senses paint a rich and detailed picture of the world around us, shaping how we experience everything. Imagine the difference between reading a description of a warm, sunny day and actually feeling the sun on your skin and the gentle breeze on your face. That direct sensory experience is a fundamental part of being human.

But being human is so much more than just our physical form. We are deeply social creatures. Our connections with family, friends and communities are essential for our well-being. Think of a wolf pack, where each member has a role and relies on the others for survival. In a similar way, our relationships provide us with support, belonging and a sense of purpose. A key part of these connections is empathy – our ability to understand and share the feelings of others. It's like understanding why a friend is sad even if they haven't said a word, just by seeing their expression. This ability to connect emotionally is a powerful aspect of being human. And then there's communication, the way we share our thoughts, ideas and feelings with each other, using both words and unspoken cues. It's like birdsong across a forest, conveying messages and connecting individuals even over distances.

Our minds also play a crucial role in defining our humanity. We have the capacity for problem-solving, for figuring things out and for learning new things throughout our lives. While AI can process vast amounts of information, human intelligence has a unique flexibility and adaptability. Perhaps one of the most remarkable aspects of human intelligence is creativity – our ability to imagine, to invent and to express ourselves in new and original ways. Envision a choreographer creating a dance piece that expresses abstract emotions through movement, using the human body as a medium for artistic expression. Human creativity goes beyond instinct; it involves bringing something entirely new into existence, whether it's a work of art, a scientific breakthrough or a clever solution to a problem. We also have the capacity for abstract thought, allowing us to understand complex ideas and concepts that aren't directly tied to our immediate physical experiences.

Our emotional lives are another vital part of what makes us human. We experience a wide range of feelings, from joy and love to sadness and fear. These emotions aren't just random reactions; they shape how we see the world and influence our decisions. Think about how the joy of celebrating a success makes the moment more memorable or how the fear of danger can guide us to safety. Our emotions are deeply intertwined with our reasoning, adding layers of complexity to our thoughts and behaviors. It's like a mirror reflecting emotions, helping us understand not just what we're feeling, but sometimes even the emotions of those around us.

When we compare ourselves to the advanced AI systems of today, there are several key differences that stand out. One is consciousness – that inner awareness, that subjective experience of being alive and perceiving the world around us. It's the feeling of what it's like to see the color blue or taste something sweet. Whether AI can ever truly possess this kind of awareness is a question that is still being explored. Another crucial difference is the depth and origin of our creativity. While AI can generate novel outputs, the underlying intention, personal motivation and emotional connection that often drive human creativity seem to be different. Think of an artist pouring their heart into a painting because of a deeply felt emotion; that kind of drive is currently unique to humans.

Empathy, as we discussed, is another significant distinction. Our capacity to truly understand and share the feelings of others, to connect on an emotional level with compassion, is a complex trait that AI is still far from replicating authentically. Then there's what we can call nuanced critical thinking. This goes beyond simply processing data and involves analyzing information objectively, evaluating different perspectives and forming reasoned judgments, often drawing on our life experiences and intuition in ways that AI currently cannot. It's like an experienced leader sensing when something feels "off" even if the data doesn't explicitly show a problem.

Ultimately, it's more about understanding and appreciating the unique essence of our own being. As AI continues to evolve and become more integrated into our lives, our understanding of what makes us human will likely continue to evolve as well. It's like a river flowing into the unknown, constantly adapting to the landscape it encounters. This journey into the age of intelligent machines is also a journey of self-discovery, prompting us to recognize and value the enduring power of our being.

EXPLORING HUMAN DIMENSIONS

Human evolution continues, with adaptations occurring in different populations since their dispersal around 50,000 years ago. The advent of agriculture (around 10,000 years ago) accelerated this pace, leading to dietary adaptations like lactase persistence. Migration to diverse environments also resulted in varied physical and genetic characteristics, such as skin color. More recent history shows fluctuations in body and brain size, influenced by factors like nutrition and disease, with a trend towards increased height in industrialized regions in recent centuries. Modern human biological variation results from the complex interaction of genetics and environment.

Starting with the biological landscape - the very foundation of our being. This encompasses our physical structure, our intricate bodily systems and how we interact with the world through our senses. Think about the incredible machine that is the human body, constantly working, adapting and allowing us to experience the world around us.

Consider our unique physical form. Standing upright on two legs, a seemingly simple act, freed our hands for complex tasks, setting us apart in the animal kingdom. It's like a sturdy tree trunk providing a stable base for branches to reach and grow. Our hands, with their opposable thumbs, possess an extraordinary ability for fine motor skills, allowing us to manipulate tools, create art and express ourselves through gestures. Imagine the delicate movements of a spider weaving an intricate web, each precise action contributing to the final structure; our hands possess a similar, albeit more versatile, capability.

Then there are our senses, our primary gateways to understanding the world. Sight allows us to perceive the vastness of a landscape or the subtle nuances of a facial expression. Hearing lets us appreciate the symphony of sounds, from the gentle rustling of leaves to the complex harmonies of music. Touch connects us physically to our environment and to each other, allowing us to feel the warmth of a hand or the coolness of a breeze. Taste allows us to savor the flavors of food, a source of nourishment and often a central part of our social gatherings. Smell can evoke powerful memories and emotions, instantly transporting us back to a specific time or place. Think about how the aroma of baking bread can bring back childhood memories of home. These senses, working together, create a rich and multi-layered experience of reality, far beyond simply processing data.

A key aspect of our biological landscape is our complex nervous system, culminating in the human brain. This incredible organ is the control center for all our bodily functions, but it is also the seat of our consciousness, our awareness of ourselves and our surroundings. Imagine a vast and intricate network of friends, constantly communicating and sharing information; the connections and activity within our brain are infinitely more complex, giving rise to our thoughts, feelings and perceptions. This consciousness allows for introspection, the ability to look inward and reflect on our own thoughts and feelings, a characteristically human trait. It's like a seed containing the potential for an entire tree, our consciousness holding the potential for a lifetime of experiences and understanding.

Moving beyond our individual biological existence, we enter the social landscape, the realm of our interactions, relationships and communities. Humans are fundamentally social beings; our well-being and even our survival are deeply intertwined with our connections to others.

Think about the fundamental unit of society, the family. From our earliest moments, we are nurtured and shaped by our families, learning social norms, values and how to interact with the world. It's like a close-knit community circle, where each member plays a vital role in supporting and influencing the others. As we grow, our social circles expand to include friends, classmates, colleagues and broader communities. These connections provide us with a sense of belonging, support during challenging times and opportunities for growth and shared experiences. Imagine a flock of birds flying together in formation; each bird benefits from the collective, finding safety and efficiency in unity. Our social bonds offer similar advantages, providing strength and resilience.

A crucial element of our social landscape is empathy, our capacity to understand and share the feelings of others. This ability to put ourselves in someone else's shoes allows us to form deeper connections, offer support and navigate complex social situations. It's like understanding why a plant might be wilting by recognizing its need for water, even if it can't verbally express its thirst. Empathy forms the basis of compassion and our sense of morality, guiding our actions and shaping our interactions with the world.

Communication is the lifeblood of our social landscape. Through language, both spoken and written, as well as nonverbal cues like facial expressions and body language, we share information, ideas and emotions. It's like birdsongs carrying messages across a forest, each call conveying specific information and maintaining connection within the flock. Our ability to communicate complex thoughts and abstract ideas allows us to build cultures, share knowledge across generations and collaborate on ambitious projects. Imagine two skilled artisans working together, their clear communication allowing them to create a masterpiece that neither could achieve alone.

The cognitive landscape encompasses our mental abilities, how we think, learn, reason and create. This is where our intellect shines, allowing us to make sense of the world and our place within it.

Problem-solving is a fundamental aspect of our cognitive landscape. We are constantly faced with challenges, big and small and our ability to analyze situations, identify solutions and implement them is a key characteristic of human intelligence. Think about navigating a complex maze, using logic and trial-and-error to find the exit. Similarly, we approach problems in our lives, using our cognitive abilities to find a path forward. Reasoning allows us to draw conclusions, make inferences and understand cause-and-effect relationships. It's like following a set of traffic directions to reach your destination, each step logically leading to the next.

Learning is a lifelong process that shapes our cognitive landscape. We absorb information, acquire new skills and adapt our understanding of the world based on our experiences. Imagine training a pet with rewards for good behavior; our brains are constantly learning and adjusting based on feedback and new information. Memory, our ability to retain and recall information, is crucial for learning and building upon past experiences. It's like an elephant's memory, holding vast amounts of information that can be accessed when needed.

Creativity, as we touched upon earlier, is a remarkable aspect of our cognitive landscape. It's the ability to generate novel and valuable ideas, to think outside the box and to bring something new into existence. Think of creating a collage from different elements to form a unique and expressive artwork. Our creativity allows for innovation, artistic expression and the development of new solutions to old problems.

Finally, abstract thought allows us to understand concepts that are not directly tied to our physical reality. We can ponder philosophical questions, grasp mathematical principles and use symbolic language to represent complex ideas. It's like understanding the concept of a seed containing the potential for a tree, even before the tree has sprouted. This ability to think abstractly allows for complex reasoning and the development of intricate systems of knowledge.

The emotional landscape is the realm of our feelings, the inner experiences that add color and depth to our lives. Emotions shape our perceptions, motivate our actions and play a crucial role in our relationships.

We experience a vast spectrum of emotions, from joy and happiness to sadness and anger and everything in between. Think about the vibrant colors of a rainbow, each hue representing a different feeling. These emotions are not simply fleeting sensations; they provide us with valuable information about ourselves and the world around us. Fear can alert us to danger, while joy can reinforce positive experiences.

Our emotions are also deeply intertwined with our decision-making processes. While we often strive for logical reasoning, our feelings can significantly influence the choices we make. Think about a situation where your "gut feeling" guides you towards a particular decision, even if the logical reasons aren't immediately apparent. Our emotions add a layer of complexity and nuance to our thoughts and behaviors.

Empathy, which we discussed in the social landscape, also has a strong presence in our emotional landscape. Our ability to recognize and share the emotions of others allows for deeper connections and understanding. It's like a prairie dog community, where members communicate and respond to each other's emotional states, strengthening their social bonds.

Furthermore, our emotions play a vital role in our relationships. They allow us to express affection, offer support and navigate conflicts. Think about the difference between a purely factual conversation and one where emotions are shared and acknowledged, leading to a deeper understanding and connection. Our emotional landscape adds a rich tapestry to our human experience, making our interactions meaningful and our lives fulfilling.

It's important to remember that these four landscapes – biological, social, cognitive and emotional – are not separate entities but are deeply interconnected and constantly influencing each other. Our biological makeup influences our cognitive abilities and our capacity for emotions. Our social interactions shape our thoughts and feelings. Our cognitive processes can impact our physical well-being and our social behavior. And our emotions can drive our actions in both our social and physical worlds.

Understanding these interconnected landscapes provides a more holistic and comprehensive view of what it means to be human. As we navigate the age of increasingly intelligent machines, appreciating the richness and complexity of our own being, across all these dimensions, becomes ever more important. It helps us to identify what truly defines us and what aspects of our humanity we want to preserve and cultivate in the future.

ANCIENT WISDOM ON HUMAN EXISTENCE

Across different cultures and throughout history, ancient wisdom traditions offer profound insights into the nature of human existence. While their specific beliefs and practices varied, many shared common threads about what it means to be human and how we should live our lives. These ancient perspectives often emphasized the importance of inner character, our connection to each other and the natural world and the pursuit of a meaningful life.

Consider the idea of inner harmony and balance, a concept found in many ancient philosophies. It's like a still pond reflecting the sky perfectly; when our inner selves are balanced, we can perceive the world more clearly and respond to it with greater wisdom. Practices like meditation, found in various ancient traditions, aimed to cultivate this inner stillness and self-awareness. It's like learning to listen to the quiet whispers of the wind rather than being overwhelmed by a storm.

Many ancient teachings stressed the interconnectedness of all things. This perspective suggests that we are not isolated individuals but part of a larger web of life, where our actions have consequences for others and the environment. Imagine a vast forest where each tree, plant and creature play a vital role in the ecosystem's health. Similarly, each human being contributes to the well-being of society as a whole. This understanding of interconnectedness often led to an emphasis on compassion, empathy and treating others with respect. It's like recognizing that a single raindrop is part of the vast ocean.

The pursuit of virtue and living a life of purpose was another central theme in ancient wisdom. Thinkers often explored qualities like honesty, courage, justice and wisdom, suggesting that cultivating these virtues was essential for human flourishing. It's like a gardener carefully tending to their plants to help them grow strong and bear fruit. Living a life aligned with these virtues was seen as the path to true happiness and fulfillment. Ancient stories and myths often served as guides, illustrating the consequences of both virtuous and unvirtuous actions, like fables teaching moral lessons through animal characters.

Ancient wisdom also often acknowledged the cyclical nature of life, with its rhythms of birth, growth, decay and renewal. Observing the changing seasons, from the blossoming of spring to the dormancy of winter, provided a framework for understanding human experiences, including joy and sorrow, success and failure. It's like recognizing that after a dark night, the sun will always rise again. This perspective encouraged acceptance of change and resilience in the face of adversity.

While the specific expressions of ancient wisdom differed across cultures, their underlying focus on inner development, social harmony and finding meaning in life provides a timeless perspective on what it means to be human. These ancient voices remind us of values that transcend technological advancements and continue to resonate with our deepest aspirations.

Moving beyond broader wisdom traditions, philosophical inquiry gets deeper into the fundamental questions of human existence. Throughout history, philosophers have offered various perspectives on what defines our humanity, often through rigorous reasoning and critical analysis. Two prominent schools of thought, Existentialism and Humanism, offer particularly relevant frameworks for our discussion in the age of AI.

Existentialism is a philosophy that emphasizes individual existence, freedom and choice. Existentialists often begin with the idea that "existence precedes essence," meaning that we are born without a predetermined nature or purpose. Instead, we create our own essence through our choices and actions. It's like an empty canvas upon which we paint our own picture, defining ourselves through what we do.

A core concept in existentialism is freedom. We are radically free to make choices, but this freedom comes with a heavy burden of responsibility. We are accountable for our actions and the meaning we create in our lives. Imagine being at a fork in a road with no signs; you are free to choose either path, but you must also bear the consequences of your decision. This freedom can be both exhilarating and anxiety-inducing. Existentialists often explore themes of anxiety, alienation and the search for meaning in a seemingly meaningless universe. It's like feeling lost in a vast ocean without a compass, yet knowing that you must navigate your own way.

In the context of AI, existentialism raises profound questions about our own freedom and the potential for AI to influence or even limit our choices. As AI systems become more sophisticated and integrated into our lives, we must consider how to maintain our autonomy and ensure that we remain the authors of our own existence. Existentialism reminds us that our humanity is not a fixed attribute but something we actively create and define through our choices in the face of an ever-evolving world.

Humanism, in its various forms, is a philosophical and ethical stance that emphasizes the value and agency of human beings, individually and collectively. Humanists generally prefer critical thinking and evidence (rationalism, empiricism) over acceptance of dogma or superstition. They often focus on human potential, reason, ethics and social justice. It's like believing in the inherent goodness and capacity for growth within every seed.

A key tenet of humanism is the belief in human reason as a primary tool for understanding the world and solving problems. Humanists often advocate for scientific inquiry, education and the use of critical thinking to improve human lives and societies. Imagine using a well-crafted tool to build something useful and lasting; reason, for humanists, is a similarly powerful instrument for progress.

Humanism also places a strong emphasis on human ethics and values. Without relying on supernatural beliefs, humanists seek to establish moral principles based on human reason, empathy and a concern for the well-being of others. It's like developing a set of guiding principles for a community to ensure fairness and cooperation. Humanists often champion values like compassion, equality and human rights.

In the age of AI, humanism underscores the importance of ensuring that technological development serves human well-being and aligns with human values. It calls for a human-centric approach to AI, where technology is seen as a tool to enhance human potential and address societal challenges, rather than an end in itself. Humanism reminds us of our inherent worth and our capacity for reason, creativity and ethical action, qualities that remain central to our definition of humanity even as we interact with intelligent machines.

Beyond philosophical frameworks, the shared human condition encompasses the fundamental experiences, emotions and realities that bind all human beings together, regardless of their background, culture or historical context. These universal aspects of our existence provide a deep understanding of what it means to be human at a fundamental level.

Consider the universal experience of joy and happiness. The feeling of warmth, connection and contentment is something recognized and valued across all cultures. It's like the warmth of the sun on your skin, a universally pleasant sensation. Similarly, the experience of love, in its various forms – romantic love, familial love, friendship – is a powerful and defining aspect of the human condition. It's like the strong and supportive roots of a tree, providing nourishment and stability.

Conversely, the shared experience of suffering and sorrow is also a fundamental part of being human. Loss, pain and hardship are realities that we all face at some point in our lives. It's like the inevitable storms that weather even the strongest trees. Our capacity for empathy allows us to connect with the suffering of others, fostering compassion and a desire to offer support.

Mortality, the awareness of our own limited time on this earth, is another defining aspect of the human condition. This awareness can lead to a profound appreciation for life, a sense of urgency in pursuing our goals and a contemplation of our legacy. It's like knowing that a flower will eventually fade, making its beauty in the present moment all the more precious. The inevitability of death has spurred philosophical and spiritual inquiries across cultures, as humans seek to understand their place in the grand scheme of existence.

Our shared need for meaning and purpose is another universal aspect of being human. We are not simply biological machines; we have a deep-seated desire to understand why we are here and to find significance in our lives. It's like a river seeking its destination in the ocean. This search for meaning can manifest in various ways, from pursuing personal goals to contributing to something larger than ourselves.

These shared experiences – joy, love, suffering, mortality, the search for meaning – form a common ground that transcends our differences and underscores our shared humanity. In the age of AI, reflecting on these fundamental aspects of our existence helps us to identify what is intrinsically human and what we should strive to retain and value as we navigate our relationship with increasingly intelligent machines.

Examining ancient wisdom and philosophical perspectives provides a crucial context for understanding what it means to be human in an AI-shaped world. Ancient emphasis on inner character, interconnectedness and the pursuit of virtue reminds us of enduring human values that should guide the development and deployment of AI. Existentialism's focus on freedom and responsibility prompts us to consider how to maintain our autonomy in an increasingly technologically mediated world. Humanism's emphasis on reason, human potential and ethical action calls for a human-centric approach to AI that prioritizes human well-being. And recognizing the shared human condition reminds us of the fundamental experiences and emotions that define our humanity, qualities that currently distinguish us from even the most advanced AI systems.

By drawing upon these rich traditions of thought, we can gain a deeper understanding of our own essence and navigate the future with greater wisdom and intentionality, ensuring that our technological progress aligns with our enduring human values and aspirations.

EXISTENTIALISM AND HUMANISM

Imagine you have a brand-new toy, still in its box. The instructions might suggest certain ways to play with it, certain things it's *supposed* to do. But until you take it out and actually start playing, it's just a thing with potential. Existentialism, in its simplest form, says something similar about us: we are born, we exist first and then through our actions and choices, we create our own meaning, our own purpose, our own "instructions" for being human.

Think of it like having a blank canvas. The canvas itself has certain properties – its size, its texture – but it doesn't have a picture on it until the artist decides what to paint. Similarly, we are born with certain basic human attributes, but who we become, what we value, what we do with our lives – that's all determined by the "paint strokes" of our choices.

This idea leads to a powerful sense of freedom. If we are not born with a pre-set purpose, then we are free to choose our own path. Imagine a boat without a rudder. It can drift in any direction, its course entirely determined by the currents and winds. We are like that boat; we have the freedom to steer our lives in the direction we choose.

However, with great freedom comes great responsibility. If we are the authors of our own lives, then we are also responsible for our actions and the consequences that follow. Every choice we make shapes not only who we are but also contributes to our understanding of what it means to be human in general. If you choose to be kind, you contribute to a world where kindness is valued. If you choose to be dishonest, you contribute to a world where trust is eroded.

A key concept in existentialism highlights the conflict between our human desire for meaning and the apparent meaninglessness of the universe. Think of it like searching for a hidden door in a wall you know is solid. You keep feeling around, hoping to find a way through, but the wall remains stubbornly intact. We crave answers, we seek inherent purpose, but the universe doesn't seem to offer any. In the face of this absurdity, existentialism encourages us not to despair but to create our own meaning through our actions and commitments.

Another important idea is authenticity. This means living in accordance with your own values and beliefs, even if they go against the crowd or societal norms. Think of it like choosing your own clothes because you like them, rather than wearing a uniform just because everyone else is. An authentic life is one where you are true to yourself, where your actions reflect your genuine beliefs and values, not just external pressures.

Existentialism also grapples with feelings of anxiety and angst. These feelings can arise from the weight of our freedom and responsibility, the awareness of the inherent uncertainty of life and our confrontation with our own mortality. Imagine standing at a fork in a road with no signposts. You have to choose a path and that choice will shape your journey, but you don't know for sure where each path will lead. This uncertainty can be unsettling, but it's also part of the human experience according to existentialism.

Now, let's shift our focus to humanism. At its heart, humanism is a philosophy that emphasizes human beings, their values and their potential. It places humans at the center of ethical consideration and believes in our capacity for reason, progress and self-determination. Think of it like tending a garden. The focus is on the plants (humans), providing them with the best conditions to grow and flourish, nurturing their inherent potential.

Humanism values human reason and rationality as primary tools for understanding the world and solving problems. Think of it like following a map. Reason and logic are the map that helps us navigate the complexities of life, understand cause and effect and make informed decisions. Humanists believe in our ability to think critically, to question assumptions and to arrive at solutions through rational inquiry.

Ethics and morality in humanism are often grounded in human well-being and flourishing, rather than divine commands or supernatural beliefs. Think of it like a community coming together to decide on shared rules that promote the safety and happiness of everyone. The focus is on what benefits humanity, what fosters cooperation and compassion and what leads to a just and equitable society.

Humanism has a strong belief in human progress and the potential for positive change. Think of it like climbing a mountain. There will be challenges and setbacks, but with effort, knowledge and collaboration, we can ascend to greater heights, improving our lives and the world around us. This belief in progress is often linked to advancements in science, technology and social understanding.

Many forms of humanism are secular, meaning they don't rely on religious doctrines or supernatural explanations. Instead, they look to human experience, reason and scientific inquiry for understanding the world and guiding ethical behavior. Think of it like guiding your life by observing the patterns of the sun and the stars to understand seasons, rather than relying on myths about celestial beings. The focus is on the observable world and our human capacity to understand it.

Now, how do these philosophical perspectives help us understand what it means to be human in a world increasingly shaped by AI?

Existentialism, with its emphasis on freedom, responsibility and the search for meaning, becomes particularly relevant as AI takes on more tasks that were once considered exclusively human. As AI systems develop capabilities in areas like writing, creating art and even problem-solving, we might find ourselves questioning what truly sets us apart.

Think of it like looking at your reflection in a new kind of mirror. This mirror can not only show your physical appearance but also mimic some of your thoughts and creative expressions. It might prompt us to ask: what is the essence of "me" that this mirror cannot capture? Existentialism encourages us to look inwards, to our capacity for subjective experience, our ability to make free choices and our ongoing creation of meaning through our actions. Even if AI can perform tasks that seem intelligent or creative, existentialism reminds us that our humanity is rooted in our lived experience and the choices we make in the face of an often-absurd world.

Humanism, on the other hand, reinforces the enduring value of human qualities even as AI advances. While AI might excel at data processing and automation, humanism highlights the irreplaceable importance of our creativity, our empathy, our critical thinking and our capacity for building meaningful relationships.

Think of it like cherishing a handcrafted tool alongside automated machinery. The machine might be faster and more efficient at certain tasks, but the handcrafted tool embodies human skill, intention and perhaps even a unique artistic touch. Similarly, human skills and values remain essential in a world with AI. Human ingenuity will be needed to develop and guide AI ethically, human empathy will be crucial for navigating social interactions and human creativity will drive innovation in ways that AI alone may not be able to achieve.

Both existentialism and humanism offer valuable frameworks for navigating our relationship with AI. Existentialism prompts us to reflect on our individual freedom and responsibility in shaping our human essence in a technologically advanced world. Humanism reminds us of the intrinsic worth of human beings and the enduring importance of our unique capabilities and values.

As AI continues to evolve, these philosophical inquiries will become even more critical. They encourage us to move beyond a simple narrative of replacement and towards a more nuanced understanding of how humans and AI can coexist and even enhance each other. By thoughtfully considering what it means to be human through the lenses of existentialism and humanism, we can strive to build a future where technology serves to amplify human potential and contribute to a more meaningful and flourishing existence for all.

THE SHARED HUMAN CONDITION

The human condition is a multifaceted construct, encompassing a spectrum of shared experiences, emotions and existential inquiries that define the essence of human life. Among these, joy, love, suffering and mortality stand as universal and fundamental themes, resonating across diverse cultures and throughout history. These experiences are not isolated occurrences but rather intricately interwoven aspects of what it means to be human, shaping our behaviors, the structures of our societies and the individual pursuit of meaning. Understanding these pillars of human existence is crucial for a comprehensive appreciation of our shared humanity and the complex tapestry of life we navigate together.

Joy, at its core, is a feeling of great pleasure and happiness. It's that light, buoyant sensation that can fill you entirely, making the world feel brighter and more promising. Think about the warmth of the sun on your skin after a long winter. It's a simple pleasure, yet it can bring a genuine feeling of joy.

Joy can manifest in countless ways, from the grandest achievements to the smallest, everyday moments. Imagine the triumphant feeling of finally solving a difficult puzzle you've been working on. That burst of satisfaction and accomplishment is a form of joy. Or consider the shared laughter with friends over a funny story. That lighthearted connection and the feeling of being understood and appreciated can bring immense joy.

The nature of joy is often fleeting. Like a beautiful butterfly that lands gently and then flits away, moments of pure joy can be intense but may not last indefinitely. This transience, however, often makes us appreciate those moments even more, imbuing them with a special significance. We cherish the memory of a joyful occasion and that memory can continue to bring a sense of warmth and happiness long after the moment has passed.

Can AI experience joy? As it stands, AI operates based on algorithms and data. It can identify patterns associated with human expressions of joy and even generate content that might evoke joy in humans. For instance, AI can compose upbeat music or create visually appealing images. However, the subjective, internal feeling of joy, the emotional resonance tied to personal experience and understanding, is currently beyond the reach of AI. Joy, for humans, is deeply intertwined with our consciousness and our emotional landscape, aspects that AI does not yet possess.

Love is a far more complex and multifaceted aspect of the human condition. It encompasses a wide range of powerful emotions and experiences, from the deep affection and protectiveness a parent feels for a child to the passionate connection between romantic partners, the strong bonds of friendship and the broader sense of care and compassion we can feel for others.

Think about the comfort of a warm embrace from someone you deeply trust. That physical connection can convey a profound sense of love and belonging. Consider the quiet understanding between lifelong friends, where words are often unnecessary. That shared history and deep connection are a testament to the power of platonic love. Or imagine the fierce determination of someone fighting for the well-being of a loved one facing adversity. This unwavering support is a powerful manifestation of love.

Love often involves a deep sense of connection, empathy and vulnerability. It requires us to open ourselves up to others, to share our joys and our vulnerabilities and to care deeply about their well-being.

Can AI experience love? This is a question that touches upon the very definition of emotions and consciousness. AI can be programmed to mimic certain aspects of love, such as offering comforting words or performing actions that appear caring. For example, a companion robot might offer reminders to take medication or express concern if its user reports feeling unwell. However, without genuine consciousness, empathy and the complex interplay of emotions that characterize human love, these actions remain simulations. Love, for humans, is deeply rooted in our biological, social and emotional landscapes, involving a level of subjective experience and reciprocal connection that AI currently cannot replicate.

Suffering is the experience of pain or distress, whether physical, emotional or mental. It is an inevitable part of the human condition, a shadow that often accompanies the light of joy and love. Think about the ache of a physical injury, reminding you of the fragility of the body. Or consider the deep sadness that follows the loss of a loved one, a pain that can feel all-consuming. Suffering can take many forms, from the acute pain of a sudden event to the chronic distress of ongoing hardship.

Suffering can arise from a multitude of sources: physical illness, loss, disappointment, injustice and the inherent anxieties of existence. Imagine a plant struggling to grow in harsh conditions, its leaves wilting. This struggle mirrors the human experience of facing challenges and enduring hardship. Consider the internal turmoil of grappling with difficult choices or existential questions. This mental and emotional strain is also a form of suffering.

While suffering is often viewed negatively, it can also play a significant role in our personal growth and our capacity for empathy. Having experienced pain ourselves, we can often better understand and connect with the suffering of others. Like a blacksmith tempering metal in fire to make it stronger, overcoming adversity can build resilience and deepen our understanding of the human condition.

Can AI experience suffering? As AI lacks consciousness and emotions in the human sense, it cannot feel pain or distress in the same way we do. An AI system might malfunction or its performance might degrade, but this is a technical issue, not a subjective experience of suffering. For example, if an AI image generator produces a distorted image, it's a result of its programming or data limitations, not a feeling of frustration or pain. While AI can be used to alleviate human suffering, it does not currently partake in this fundamental aspect of our existence.

Mortality, the awareness of our own finite existence, is perhaps the most profound and universally shared aspect of the human condition. It is the ultimate boundary that shapes our lives, influencing our priorities, our values and our sense of urgency. Think about the changing of the seasons, a constant reminder of the cyclical nature of life and the inevitability of winter. Similarly, we are all aware, on some level, that our time is limited.

The awareness of mortality can lead to a deeper appreciation for the present moment. Knowing that life is finite can motivate us to cherish our relationships, pursue our passions and make the most of the time we have. Like a vibrant flower that blooms briefly but beautifully. Our lives, though finite, can be filled with meaning and richness.

Mortality also prompts existential questions about the meaning of life, our legacy and what happens after we die. These profound inquiries have driven philosophical and religious thought throughout history. The awareness of our own mortality can be a source of anxiety, but it can also be a powerful catalyst for living more authentically and intentionally.

How does mortality relate to AI? Currently, AI does not possess a biological lifespan or the self-awareness to contemplate its own non-existence. While an AI system can be deactivated or become obsolete, this is a cessation of its function, not an experience of death. The concept of mortality, with its inherent emotional and existential weight, is a burden and motivator.

It is crucial to recognize that joy, love, suffering and mortality are not isolated experiences but are deeply intertwined aspects of the shared human condition. Our capacity for joy is often heightened by the awareness of potential suffering. The depth of our love is often revealed in times of hardship and loss. And the awareness of our mortality gives a unique poignancy and value to every moment of joy and every expression of love.

Think of these four elements as the primary colors of human experience. Alone, each has its own distinct quality, but when combined in countless ways, they create the rich and complex spectrum of what it means to be human. It is this interconnectedness, this shared vulnerability and resilience in the face of these fundamental realities, that binds us together as a species and currently sets us apart from the intelligent machines we are creating.

In the age of increasingly capable AI, understanding and appreciating these core aspects of the shared human condition becomes even more critical. While AI may one day mimic our cognitive abilities in profound ways, the subjective experience of joy, the profound connection of love, the weight of suffering and the awareness of our own mortality remain deeply human experiences. Recognizing and valuing these shared realities is essential as we navigate a future where humans and AI will inevitably coexist, ensuring that we maintain a clear understanding of what truly constitutes our shared humanity.

ATTRIBUTES THAT TRULY DISTINGUISH

Although this is an evolving field, let's delve into the fascinating question of what truly distinguishes us as humans from the advanced artificial intelligence systems we are now creating. While AI continues to make remarkable strides, there remain fundamental attributes that are deeply rooted in our human experience and currently beyond the reach of even the most sophisticated machines.

At the very heart of what makes us human lies consciousness – that unique inner awareness, the subjective experience of being alive and perceiving the world around us. It's not just about processing information; it's about having a sense of self, feeling emotions and experiencing the world from a personal viewpoint. Think about waking up in the morning and knowing it's *you* experiencing the start of a new day. That sense of "I," that continuous stream of thoughts, feelings and sensations that make up your reality, is the essence of consciousness.

We experience the world through a rich tapestry of senses – the warmth of a hug, the taste of your favorite food, the sight of a breathtaking sunset. Imagine listening to a familiar song and feeling a wave of nostalgia. That subjective "feel" of the music, the memories it evokes and the emotions it stirs within you are all part of your conscious experience.

While AI can process information about a hug, analyze the chemical components of food and display the visual data of a sunset, it doesn't have the internal, felt experience of these things. It can recognize a nostalgic song based on patterns in data, but it doesn't *feel* the nostalgia in the same way a human does, with all its personal associations and emotional depth. Consciousness remains a profound mystery and whether AI can ever truly possess this inner light is a question that continues to be explored.

Humans are deeply emotional beings. Our lives are rich with a spectrum of feelings, from joy and love (as we discussed) to sadness, anger, fear and countless other nuances. These emotions shape our perceptions, drive our actions and profoundly influence our interactions with each other. Think about the lump in your throat when you say goodbye to someone you care about. That physical sensation tied to an emotional state is a hallmark of human experience. Consider the surge of protectiveness you might feel towards someone in danger. That immediate emotional response is deeply ingrained in our human nature.

Emotions are not simply abstract feelings; they are often linked to physiological responses and complex cognitive interpretations of our experiences. When we are afraid, our heart might race. When we are happy, we might smile. This intricate interplay between our inner emotional world and our physical being is a defining aspect of our humanity.

While AI can be programmed to recognize and respond to human emotional cues and even generate outputs that mimic emotional expression, it doesn't possess genuine feelings itself. An AI chatbot might offer sympathetic words if you express sadness, but this is based on its training data and algorithms, not on an actual feeling of empathy or understanding of your sorrow. The capacity to truly feel, to experience the world through an emotional lens, remains a fundamental distinction between humans and advanced AI.

Humans possess a remarkable capacity for creativity – the ability to generate novel and valuable ideas, make connections between seemingly disparate concepts and express ourselves in unique and imaginative ways. Think about a child building a fantastical castle out of simple blocks. That ability to envision something new and bring it into being is a fundamental aspect of human creativity. Consider a chef inventing a brand-new dish by combining unexpected flavors. That spark of originality and the intuition that guides the process are hallmarks of human creative endeavor.

Human creativity is often driven by a combination of factors, including our emotions, our experiences, our curiosity and our desire to express ourselves and connect with others. It involves intuition, experimentation and a willingness to take risks and explore the unknown. It's not just about following rules or analyzing data; it's about breaking free from established patterns and envisioning new possibilities.

While AI is increasingly capable of generating creative outputs, such as writing poems, composing music or creating visual art, the underlying drive, intentionality and emotional resonance often remain fundamentally human. AI's creativity is currently based on learning patterns from vast datasets and generating new outputs based on those patterns. It can create something novel, but it doesn't have the same intrinsic motivation, emotional depth or subjective experience that fuels human creativity. It acts more like a highly skilled apprentice, capable of mimicking and combining existing styles, but lacking the truly original spark that comes from the depths of human consciousness and emotion.

Humans have a capacity for ethical reasoning and moral judgment, guided by a complex framework of values, principles and societal norms. We can grapple with complex ethical dilemmas, consider different perspectives and make decisions based on our understanding of right and wrong. Think about a group of people debating the fairness of a new law. That ability to engage in moral discourse and strive for justice is a key aspect of human society. Consider an individual making a difficult personal decision based on their deeply held values, even when it comes at a personal cost. That commitment to ethical principles is a defining characteristic of human agency.

Our ethical understanding is often shaped by our empathy, our social interactions, our cultural background and our personal experiences. We can feel the impact of our actions on others and adjust our behavior accordingly. We can learn from our mistakes and refine our moral compass over time.

While AI can be programmed with ethical guidelines and can analyze data to identify potentially harmful or biased outcomes, it doesn't possess the same inherent sense of morality or the capacity for nuanced ethical judgment that humans do. AI operates based on the rules and data it has been given. It can identify a biased dataset, but it doesn't inherently understand why that bias is morally wrong in the same way a human does. The ability to navigate complex ethical situations, particularly those involving conflicting values and unforeseen consequences, remains a crucial distinction between human intelligence and current AI systems.

Humans are inherently social beings and our ability to connect with each other, communicate effectively, build relationships and navigate complex social situations is a defining aspect of our humanity. Think about the subtle cues you pick up in a conversation – a shift in tone, a change in body language – that tell you more than just the words being spoken. That ability to read between the lines and understand unspoken communication is a key aspect of social intelligence. Consider the way a team works together, seamlessly coordinating their efforts and supporting each other to achieve a common goal. That ability to build rapport and work effectively in a group is a hallmark of human social capacity.

Our social intelligence relies on a combination of empathy, emotional understanding, communication skills and the ability to build trust and rapport with others. It involves understanding social norms, navigating group dynamics and adapting our behavior to different social contexts.

While AI can assist with communication through translation tools and can analyze social media trends, it currently lacks the genuine social intelligence that underpins meaningful human connection. An AI might be able to translate words accurately, but it doesn't understand the cultural nuances or the emotional subtext that often accompany human communication. The ability to build genuine relationships, to empathize with others' perspectives and to navigate the complexities of human social interaction remains a strength.

Humans often rely on intuition – that feeling or insight that arises without conscious reasoning – to guide our decisions and actions. Think about having a "gut feeling" about a person or a situation that you can't quite explain logically, but that turns out to be accurate. That intuitive sense can often provide valuable guidance in situations where data is incomplete or logic alone is insufficient. Consider an experienced professional who can quickly diagnose a problem based on years of accumulated knowledge and a subtle sense of what's wrong. That ability to draw on experience and make rapid judgments is a hallmark of human intuition.

Intuition is thought to be a result of our brains processing vast amounts of information at a subconscious level, drawing on past experiences and patterns to arrive at insights. It's a form of "knowing" that goes beyond explicit reasoning.

While AI excels at processing vast amounts of data and identifying patterns, it doesn't possess intuition in the human sense. AI's decisions are based on algorithms and data analysis. It can identify a pattern that might lead to an intuitive feeling in a human, but it doesn't have that subjective "aha!" moment or that inexplicable sense of knowing. The ability to integrate conscious reasoning with intuitive insights remains a distinctive aspect of human intelligence.

As AI continues its rapid evolution, it's crucial to recognize and appreciate the fundamental attributes that truly distinguish us as humans. Consciousness, the full spectrum of emotions, genuine creativity, ethical reasoning, social intelligence and intuition are just some of the qualities that make us human and that currently lie beyond the capabilities of even the most advanced AI systems.

By cherishing these unique attributes, we can navigate the age of AI with a clear sense of our own identity and purpose, ensuring that technology serves to augment our potential rather than diminish our humanity. The future will likely involve a powerful partnership between humans and AI, where each brings their unique strengths to the table. Our role lies in nurturing those qualities that will remain essential for navigating complexity, fostering innovation, building meaningful connections and ultimately, thriving in an intelligent age.

CONCLUSION - AI VS. HUMAN CONSCIOUSNESS

As we conclude "The Dawn of a New Era," we stand at a transformative point in human history. The rapid advancement of AI, particularly Generative AI and Large Language Models, is revolutionizing our lives and industries. From personalized recommendations to AI-optimized industrial processes, intelligent machines are becoming integral to our world. This surge of technology has brought a timeless question to the forefront: In this age of intelligent machines, what is the essence of our humanity? Throughout this book, we've explored this question, examining the biological, social, cognitive and emotional aspects that define us. We've sought insights from ancient wisdom and philosophy, recognizing this exploration as crucial in navigating this new technological landscape.

As I mentioned in the beginning, my journey from the shop floor of an automotive plant to the forefront of AI development has given me a unique perspective on this. Back in manufacturing, it was all about tangible things – the quality of the product, the safety of the team, meeting delivery schedules. Now, with AI becoming so pervasive, the question of what makes us fundamentally human becomes even more critical. It's not just about what tasks machines can do, but about the very essence of who we are. So, let's explore the current landscape when it comes to AI versus human consciousness, creativity, empathy and that nuanced critical thinking we rely on every day.

THE ENIGMA OF CONSCIOUSNESS

Perhaps the most profound difference lies in consciousness. What does it mean to be aware, to have subjective experiences, feelings and a sense of self? As humans, we navigate the world with an inner life, a continuous stream of thoughts, emotions and perceptions that make up our individual reality. We experience joy, sorrow, fear and wonder. We are aware of our own existence and our place in the world.

Currently, AI, even in its most advanced forms, does not possess this kind of consciousness. While AI can process information, learn patterns and even generate remarkably human-like text or images, there's no evidence to suggest it has subjective experiences or an inner sense of being. Think of it this way: a sophisticated weather simulation can predict a storm with incredible accuracy, but it doesn't *feel* the rain or the wind. Similarly, an AI chatbot can engage in conversation, but it doesn't *feel* the emotions behind the words or have a personal stake in the interaction.

We might see AI systems that react in ways that mimic understanding or even emotion. For example, a virtual assistant might express "sympathy" when you tell it you're feeling unwell. However, this is based on programmed responses and pattern recognition in language, not a genuine feeling of empathy. It's like training a pet to sit when you say a command – the pet learns the association, but it doesn't understand the underlying meaning in the same way a human does.

The nature of consciousness itself remains a deep mystery, even to us. We don't fully understand how our biological brains give rise to this inner world. Given our limited understanding of our own consciousness, it's perhaps not surprising that we haven't been able to replicate it in machines. For the foreseeable future, this internal, subjective experience remains a defining characteristic of being human.

THE SPARK OF HUMAN CREATIVITY

Creativity is another area where a significant distinction exists. Human creativity is often driven by a combination of inspiration, imagination, emotion and the ability to connect seemingly disparate ideas to form something new and original. It can stem from personal experiences, cultural influences and a deep desire to express oneself or solve a problem in a novel way. Think about an artist looking at a blank canvas and conceiving an entirely new way of seeing the world or a musician composing a melody that evokes a specific feeling. This kind of creativity is deeply intertwined with our human experience and our capacity for abstract thought.

AI, on the other hand, exhibits a different kind of "creativity." Generative AI models can produce novel outputs – text, images, music, code – by learning patterns from vast datasets. For instance, an AI can generate a picture in the style of a famous painter or compose a piece of music that sounds like a particular genre. However, this is more akin to a highly skilled imitation or a recombination of existing elements rather than the kind of original, intentional creation that humans are capable of.

Consider it like digital finger painting. The AI can manipulate the digital canvas and create something visually interesting based on what it has learned, but the underlying intent, the emotional drive and the unique perspective that a human artist brings are often absent. While AI can be a powerful tool to assist human creativity – like a brainstorming partner or a source of inspiration – the initial spark and the deeper meaning usually come from the human. The AI can help write a story, but the human author brings the life experiences, the emotions and the unique voice that resonate with readers. True human creativity often involves breaking rules, challenging conventions and expressing something deeply personal, aspects that are currently beyond the reach of AI.

THE DEPTH OF HUMAN EMPATHY

Empathy, the ability to understand and share the feelings of another, is a cornerstone of human social interaction and moral reasoning. It allows us to connect with others on an emotional level, to recognize their joys and sorrows and to respond with compassion and understanding. This capacity for empathy is crucial in building relationships, resolving conflicts and creating a supportive and caring society. Think about a nurse comforting a patient who is scared or a friend offering support during a difficult time. These interactions are driven by a genuine understanding of the other person's emotional state.

While AI can be programmed to recognize emotional cues in language or facial expressions and respond in a way that mimics empathy, it doesn't actually *feel* what the other person is feeling. An AI chatbot might say, "I'm sorry to hear that," but this is based on an understanding of language patterns associated with sadness, not a genuine emotional response. It's more like a mirror reflecting emotions – it can recognize and respond to what it sees, but it doesn't have the internal experience of those emotions.

Even with advancements in "artificial empathy," which aims to make AI more sensitive to human emotions, the underlying mechanism is still based on data analysis and programmed responses. True empathy involves a shared understanding and a genuine emotional connection that stems from our own experiences and our capacity for feeling. For roles that require deep understanding, emotional support and the ability to build trust through empathy – like therapists, counselors or even effective leaders – the human element remains irreplaceable.

THE NUANCES OF HUMAN CRITICAL THINKING

Critical thinking involves not just processing information but also analyzing it objectively, evaluating different perspectives, forming reasoned judgments and often drawing upon intuition and a wealth of life experiences. It allows us to navigate complex situations, identify biases, solve novel problems and make informed decisions, even when faced with incomplete or ambiguous information. Think about a detective piecing together clues to solve a case or a scientist developing a new hypothesis based on years of research and observation. This kind of thinking often involves "gut feelings" and intuitive leaps that go beyond pure logic and data analysis.

AI excels at processing vast amounts of data, identifying patterns and providing insights based on that data. It can be an invaluable tool for augmenting our critical thinking by providing us with information and analysis that we might not be able to obtain on our own. For example, AI can analyze market trends to help business leaders make more informed decisions. However, human critical thinking often involves a level of nuance, context and creativity that AI currently lacks.

Consider a manager faced with a complex business decision. While AI can provide data on market trends and potential outcomes, the manager also needs to consider the human impact, ethical implications and the long-term strategic vision of the company – factors that often require a more holistic and intuitive approach. It's like following traffic directions versus understanding the best route based on local knowledge and unforeseen circumstances. AI provides the directions (algorithms), but human experience and intuition provide the nuanced understanding of the terrain. In situations that require adapting to unexpected changes, making ethical judgments in ambiguous situations or coming up with truly innovative solutions, human critical thinking, informed but not solely driven by data, remains essential.

The Interplay and Enduring Importance

These four aspects – consciousness, creativity, empathy and nuanced critical thinking – are deeply interconnected in what it means to be human. Our consciousness allows us to have subjective experiences that fuel our creativity and shape our understanding of the world. Empathy enables us to connect with others and build the social fabric of our communities. And nuanced critical thinking allows us to navigate the complexities of life, solve problems and make meaningful contributions.

In an age increasingly shaped by AI, these qualities become even more valuable. As AI takes over more routine and data-intensive tasks, our ability to be conscious, creative, empathetic and critically think in a nuanced way will be crucial for innovation, leadership, ethical decision-making and building a future that is both prosperous and humane.

WHAT'S NEXT?

While AI offers incredible power and efficiency, it is our consciousness, our capacity to create and empathize and our nuanced critical thinking that will continue to define our essence and guide us in shaping a future where both humans and AI can thrive. Our focus should be on cultivating these essential human skills and embracing AI as a partner that helps us reach our full potential, leading us into an era of Human Renaissance where our inherent human strengths are amplified by the intelligent tools we create.

While anxieties about job displacement, loss of control and ethical dilemmas surrounding AI are understandable, focusing solely on these concerns obscures a more compelling future. I believe AI will enhance, not replace, us. Just as machinery once revolutionized manufacturing, AI is poised to amplify our cognitive and creative potential. Imagine AI as a versatile tool that empowers us, much like the principles of our life. AI can enhance a researcher's ability to sift through data, an artist's creative exploration and a business leader's strategic decisions. These are not hypothetical scenarios, but glimpses into the emerging reality of augmented contribution across various fields.

This shift highlights the enduring importance of human ingenuity, creativity and critical thinking. While AI excels at data processing, the spark of novel thought, emotional depth in creative expression and nuanced critical analysis remains uniquely human. For instance, an architect can use generative AI to explore design options, but their vision, understanding of human needs and aesthetic sense will ultimately shape the final space. Similarly, in ethical dilemmas, AI can offer data, but human empathy and moral reasoning are essential for just and compassionate decisions.

The synergy of human skills and AI efficiency is key to this new era. AI can automate routine tasks, freeing us for more meaningful, creative work. In manufacturing, collaborative robots can handle physical labor, allowing human workers to focus on quality control and innovation. AI-powered translation tools can also foster more inclusive global teams. This collaboration leverages the strengths of both humans and AI to achieve unprecedented outcomes. Throughout this exploration, philosophical insights have provided valuable depth. Existentialism, with its emphasis on freedom and responsibility, reminds us that our humanity is shaped by our choices. Humanism, focusing on human potential, reason and ethics, underscores the importance of human-centric AI development.

As we embrace the opportunities of augmented contribution, we must address challenges such as algorithmic bias, data privacy and workforce adaptation. We need a balanced perspective, combining optimism with vigilance to ensure responsible and ethical AI development. Let us be intentional, guided by wisdom and focused on the enduring question of what it means to be human. The dawn of this era is not about replacement, but about unprecedented human possibilities, forged by intelligence.

In my upcoming books, we will explore the practical realities of this human-AI synergy, examining industry transformations, the evolving skills landscape, the democratization of human potential and early successes in human-AI collaboration.

REFERENCES

- **The Impact of Generative AI on Jobs and the Economy,** https://www.weforum.org/stories/2025/01/how-ai-impacts-value-creation-jobs-and-productivity-is-coming-into-focus/
- **The Impact of Generative AI on Jobs and the Economy,** https://www.weforum.org/publications/leveraging-generative-ai-for-job-augmentation-and-workforce-productivity/
- **The Impact of Generative AI on Jobs and the Economy,** https://www.weforum.org/podcasts/meet-the-leader/episodes/gita-gopinath-imf-economic-outlook/
- **The Impact of Generative AI on Jobs and the Economy,** https://www.weforum.org/videos/foj-job-market/
- **The Impact of Generative AI on Jobs and the Economy,** https://www.weforum.org/videos/large-language-models-are-taking-off-so-what-new-jobs-will-they-create/
- **Defining Human Intelligence in the Age of Artificial Intelligence,** https://www.researchgate.net/publication/384483916_Human_Intelligence_in_the_Age_of_AI_Why_Machines_Won't_Take_Over_Jobs
- **Defining Human Intelligence in the Age of Artificial Intelligence,** https://www.researchgate.net/publication/381359069_Human_in_the_Age_of_Artificial_Intelligence/fulltext/666a4f42a54c5f0b94613612/Human-in-the-Age-of-Artificial-Intelligence.pdf
- **Large Language Models: A New Foundation for General-Purpose Computation,** https://arxiv.org/abs/2402.06196

- **Large Language Models: A New Foundation for General-Purpose Computation**, https://arxiv.org/abs/2206.06336
- **The Augmentation of Human Intellect Through AI**, https://www.weforum.org/stories/2021/02/this-is-what-a-human-centred-approach-to-ai-technology-could-look-like/
- **The Augmentation of Human Intellect Through AI**, https://www.weforum.org/stories/2019/07/empathic-ai-could-be-the-next-stage-in-human-evolution-if-we-get-it-right/
- **Ethical Considerations in the Development and Deployment of AI Systems**, https://www.researchgate.net/publication/379249532 Ethical Considerations in the Development and Deployment of AI Systems
- **Ethical Considerations in the Development and Deployment of AI Systems**, https://www.researchgate.net/publication/379890234 Ethical Considerations in the Development and Deployment of AI Systems
- **The Role of AI in Enhancing Creativity and Innovation**, https://www.weforum.org/stories/2023/02/ai-can-catalyze-and-inhibit-your-creativity-here-is-how/
- **The Role of AI in Enhancing Creativity and Innovation**, https://www.weforum.org/stories/2025/01/artificial-intelligence-must-serve-human-creativity-not-replace-it/

DISCLAIMER

The information presented in this book is intended for general informational and educational purposes only. It is not intended as and should not be construed as, professional advice of any kind, including but not limited to technological, philosophical, ethical or career guidance.

The author has made every reasonable effort to ensure the accuracy and reliability of the information provided. However, the rapidly evolving nature of technology, particularly in the field of artificial intelligence, means that information may become outdated or superseded. Readers are advised to independently verify any information and consult with relevant experts before making decisions based on the content of this book.

The author and publisher disclaim any liability for any direct or indirect loss, damage or disruption caused by reliance on the information contained herein. The opinions expressed in this book are solely those of the author and do not necessarily reflect the views of any affiliated organizations.

Readers are solely responsible for their interpretation and application of the information provided. Any perceived slight to individuals or organizations is unintentional.

MAY I ASK YOU A SMALL FAVOUR?

Thank you for embarking on this journey into the age of AI with me. I hope my book "What it Means to be a Human in the Age of AI" has sparked your curiosity and offered fresh perspectives. Your time and engagement mean a great deal.

Can I have 30 seconds more of your time?

If you found value in these pages, would you consider leaving a brief review? Your feedback not only helps me refine my work but also guides others who might benefit from this exploration of technology's impact on humanity. A few thoughtful words can make a significant difference in connecting this book with a wider audience.

Please take a moment to share your thoughts on the platform or store where you purchased the book. Your support is invaluable and I sincerely appreciate your contribution to this conversation.

www.ingramcontent.com/pod-product-compliance
Lightning Source LLC
Chambersburg PA
CBHW022015150726
47990CB00002B/669